THE
9
NATURAL
LAWS OF
LEADERSHIP

THE 9 NATURAL LAWS OF LEADERSHIP

WARREN BLANK

amacom

American Management Association

New York • Atlanta • Boston • Chicago • Kansas City • San Francisco • Washington, D.C.
Brussels • Mexico City • Tokyo • Toronto

This publication is designed to provide accurate and authoritative
information in regard to the subject matter covered. It is sold with the
understanding that the publisher is not engaged in rendering legal,
accounting, or other professional service. If legal advice or other expert
assistance is required, the services of a competent professional person
should be sought.

Library of Congress Cataloging-in-Publication Data

Blank, Warren.
    The 9 natural laws of leadership / Warren Blank.
        p.   cm.
    Includes index.
    ISBN 0-8144-0309-3
    1. Ledership.   I. Title.
    HD57.7.B565   1995
    658.4'092—dc20   95-33153
                                            CIP

Printing number

10   9   8   7   6

Contents

Preface

The Nine Natural Laws of Leadership answers the questions: What does it mean to be a leader? When and how does leadership occur? How do leaders and managers differ? What is the source of a leader's power? And, perhaps most important: How can leaders provide more enlightened, life-supporting direction for their organizations?

Answers to these questions will provide practical choices for those men and women who care to take initiative and make a difference in their organizations. A paradigm shift has occurred in our knowledge about nature's deeper realities, and that mind-set offers new insights into our understanding of leadership. This book defines a new way of thinking about leadership, describes a new leadership paradigm, and offers practical action ideas to guide leaders.

Leadership and Natural Law

After almost 100 years of formal study, leadership remains an elusive phenomenon that everyone yearns for but often finds to be in short supply. I believe the problem lies in the way people think about leadership. To date, we still do not have a complete understanding of leadership's most fundamental natural laws. By *natural law*, I mean the intelligence or order that explains the patterns of behavior and interaction of leadership. Today, people commonly view leadership by focusing only on the leader, and they commonly define leaders by their personal traits, behaviors, or habits. This approach fails to address the deeper reality: that to be a leader means to have willing followers. The focus on the leader alone obscures the interactional quality of leadership, and the obsession with individual attributes fails to recognize that such characteristics are important only in relation to followers.

The Nine Natural Laws of Leadership defines the fundamental laws that describe leaders in all contexts and across all scales—from leaders of countries and leaders of large and small companies to leaders of quality improvement teams. The nine natural laws spell out the requirements for anyone who is a leader. They show how all leaders influence others, describe the arena in which every leader operates, detail the boundary conditions and realistic consequences faced by anyone who leads, and define the source of leadership capability within each person. The nine laws also provide a practical guide for anyone who wants to take the lead.

A New Leadership Paradigm

Knowledge about any phenomenon's natural laws depends on the prevailing paradigm used to make sense of nature. The existing leadership mind-set is based on a set of assumptions developed in the seventeenth century, known as classical or Newtonian physics. For example, the repeated attempts to define leadership in terms of the leader alone and to understand leaders in terms of a set of traits or habits are based on Newton's assumption that nature is made up of separate bits of solid matter, which suggests that nature can be understood by breaking it down into its separate and independent components. Newton's approach, while valid for material objects, has not helped us to understand leadership.

The discovery of quantum physics at the beginning of the twentieth century shattered Newton's worldview as the definitive portrait of reality. Quantum physics reveals deeper layers of nature's functioning and has provided new and compelling insights into economics, technology, and psychology (e.g., George Gilder's *Microcosm: The Quantum Revolution in Economics and Technology* and Danah Zohar's *The Quantum Self: Human Nature and Consciousness Defined by the New Physics*). The quantum paradigm offers a set of assumptions that provide a more complete and appropriate understanding of leadership. For example, quantum physics explains that at the deepest levels, reality is a field, an interaction that cannot be understood in terms of separate parts.

The nine natural laws of leadership are based on these and other assumptions derived from the quantum worldview. These assumptions suggest a new mind-set, the Quantum Leadership paradigm, that offers a more compelling description of leadership.

To illustrate, Quantum Leadership explains that leadership is best understood in terms of leaders and followers together. Through the lens of Quantum Leadership we recognize that leadership is a field, an interaction, an interdependence of leaders and followers. Quantum Leadership defines the power of leadership as the connection between leaders and followers who together play a role in generating leadership power. The Quantum Leadership paradigm expands the part everyone can play in guiding an organization.

Quantum Leadership also offers guidance for leaders in today's competitive environment. Successful businesses cannot compete using a fragmented approach. The global competitive environment is best understood as a total field. Quantum Leadership shows leaders how to be "field conscious" and to have a broad perspective of the larger competitive field while maintaining a sharp focus on localized interactions.

This book describes the Quantum Leadership paradigm and offers a model for guiding leadership action. The model explains how leaders recognize solutions to problems and take advantage of opportunities. The model defines how leaders perform actions that enlighten followers to join the leader. At the foundation of the model is the key to reinforcing and developing more enlightened, life-supporting leaders. Quantum Leadership recognizes that consciousness, how people process information, creates leadership. Quantum Leadership directs people to expand their consciousness so that they can overcome the limitations and destructive biases that result in life-damaging or mistake-ridden leadership action. With greater self-awareness, Quantum Leaders can harness the full power of leadership and use that power in a more enlightened way.

Practical Action Ideas

The Natural Laws of Leadership offers more than 150 practical action ideas to guide leaders. These action ideas are not absolutes that guarantee specific results in a particular circumstance. Newton's cause-and-effect determinism does not fit the reality of leading. The action ideas reflect the quantum assumption that probabilities, nonlinearity, and uncertainty characterize the leader's arena of action. They provide possibilities to consider and experiment with as part of the artful application of leadership.

The action ideas provide choices designed to increase your arsenal of potential ways to succeed. Some may not appeal to you; ignore them in favor of those you do like. There will be situations when it is not possible to try certain action ideas; focus on those you *can* use and do not get mired in what cannot be done. Some action ideas may be easier to apply than others; work on implementing a range of actions from easy to more difficult so that you stretch your capacity. Some action ideas will work in one circumstance and not in another; avoid becoming robotic and assuming that what worked once will always work in the future. Learn from the implementation of every action idea.

Overview of Chapters

Chapter 1 provides a brief case study to illustrate how we typically think about leadership and to show the limitations of traditional views.

Chapter 2 spells out the nine natural laws of leadership.

Chapter 3 describes the Quantum Leadership paradigm by contrasting the five assumptions of the traditional classical physics leadership mind-set with the five assumptions of the quantum view. The chapter also describes how Quantum Leadership is more appropriate for modern organizations than classical leadership.

Chapter 4 presents the Quantum Leadership model and describes how it fits today's competitive conditions. It also details how it offers a useful guide for more enlightened leadership.

Chapter 5 describes the Quantum Leader within, our capacity to use our mind or consciousness, and the four quantum powers of consciousness.

Chapter 6 details how Quantum Leaders identify problems and possibilities and define courses of action to solve problems and exploit opportunities. Quantum Leaders perceive what others don't—they recognize events and process information that others overlook or ignore.

Chapter 7 explains how Quantum Leaders go into The G.A.P., the place where they gain another perspective, to break the boundaries that limit, bias, or distort perception and to open themselves to new ways of observing, interpreting, and evaluating information.

Chapter 8 describes how Quantum Leaders gain commitment from followers through influence tactics that enlighten followers so that they perceive the merit of the leader and the leader's course of action.

Chapter 9 presents how Quantum Leaders create shared meaning, the connection that attracts followers. Quantum Leaders match the follower's values and reframe information so that followers can understand and accept the leader's message.

Chapter 10 offers ways Quantum Leaders influence others on the subtlest levels of information processing. People have internal codes or a private mental language they use to create meaning. Quantum Leaders speak this language to influence followers.

Chapter 11 explains how Quantum Leaders cultivate relationships with others so that they are more likely to follow.

Chapter 12 differentiates leaders from managers by explaining how leaders are better understood through a quantum approach and how managers are more clearly perceived through the lens of classical physics.

The final chapter explains how to develop Quantum Leaders by expanding consciousness, the fundamental source of leadership, so that leaders can fulfill the possibilities of leading.

A Personal Perspective

I believe that every person has the capacity to lead. Some people may lead in the worldscape theater of business or international politics or in the arenas of global health of education. Others may lead in small groups or one-to-one interactions. In every case, the mechanics or science of leadership is the same. This book describes that science in terms of the nine natural laws and the Quantum Leadership paradigm.

Furthermore, leaders at all levels and in all arenas must be artful in their implementation of the science. This requires the expansion of consciousness. The Quantum Leadership paradigm describes the tools for doing so.

Consciousness is the one indispensable ingredient that establishes the basis for enlightened leadership. By expanding consciousness, the Quantum Leader's relationship to the world changes at the fundamental level of mind. With expanded consciousness the Quantum Leader has the solid intention to lead, the highly focused attention needed to resolve problems and exploit opportunities, the refined discrimination to consider more choices and interpret choices in more constructive ways, and the driving initiative to take positive action.

The German philosopher Goethe wrote:

> "If I accept you as you are, I will make you worse; however, if I treat you as though you are what you are capable of becoming, I help you become that."

I hope this book helps each reader enliven the consciousness within him or herself to become a life-supporting Quantum Leader.

Acknowledgments

At the deepest layers of reality, everything is connected. Existence displays itself as fields of interaction, which is why this book could never have been written without the insights and support of many individuals.

First, I want to thank the thousands of participants in my leadership training seminars who asked so many penetrating questions about practical issues and challenged me to think through my ideas about leadership.

And I would specifically like to thank all those who allowed me to recount their personal leadership experiences: Ray Alvord, David Bell, Dick Frazar, Ron Fisher, Joe Frick, Pat Grysavage, Martha Hahn, Dudley Hanson, Joseph Hoeg, Floyd Hoelting, Louis Katopodis, John Lainhart, Leon Moore, Garry Nelson, Robert Nelson, Ron Opitz, and Alex Stolley.

I also want to thank Terry Fairchild for his help with earlier versions of the manuscript, and the staff at AMACOM, particularly Adrienne Hickey and Kate Pferdner.

I am indebted to Steven G. Green, an outstanding leadership scholar and good friend, for all he has taught me about leadership.

My deepest gratitude goes to M. for providing me with knowledge about the meaning of life.

To my mother, Helen, thank you for being a model of someone who is always learning and growing.

And to the most important person in my life, my wife, Mary Ann Cooke: Thank you for being my perfect partner.

1

In Search of Leadership

"Leadership, I'm not sure how to define it, but I know it when I see it."

—*Dwight David Eisenhower, U.S. president and five-star general*

Leadership. The word inspires images that range from a power for positive change to a force that can misdirect to a capacity that is often absent when we need it most. To fulfill the search for leadership we need to examine what we believe represents leadership and why.

Who Is the Leader?

Everyone sitting at the large conference table wonders what will happen now that Tom Hammonds, Chem-Labs' dynamic founder and vigorous, hands-on president, is in the hospital. He will survive the massive stroke suffered seventy-two hours ago, but he remains in a coma and it is unclear when or if he will regain his full faculties.

The stroke was completely unexpected. Hammonds had not even considered the need to mold a successor, thinking there would be plenty of time for that later.

Hushed, anxious comments pass among the twenty-three Chem-Labs managers, supervisors, and senior-level employees. Then Barry Sherman, the longest-tenured of Chem-Labs' four managers, stands and addresses the group. "This news is a severe blow," he states, "but

1

we have to remain calm. We have to stay on track. I am sure things will work out."

Barry stops as the president's secretary quickly enters the room and hands him a fax. "This just came in from Beijing, the China group," she says in a quiet, nervous tone. "I realized I had to show it to somebody."

The words **Beijing** and **China** *create a stir. For nine months, Hammonds had worked on establishing a market in China. The move was expected to more than double Chem-Labs' revenues over the next three years, and to serve as a springboard for international expansion into the entire Pacific Rim.*

"What does the fax say?" Helen Gitler, Chem-Lab's newest manager asks.

"The consortium expresses their condolences and wishes Tom Hammonds a speedy recovery," Barry says. "They then state, 'Due to these unfortunate circumstances, we need to reevaluate our position regarding our joint business venture.' "

Statements of disbelief, anger, and uncertainty erupt from the group. "This can't be!" "Damn! How can they do this now?" "First, Tom, now this. What else will go wrong?"

Barry waves a hand and says, "Okay. Let's remain calm. This isn't our only important deal."

"Well, what does it mean?" *one of the senior employees asks.*

"Have we lost the deal completely?" *another queries.*

"No one can be sure," Helen declares. "We need more information."

Bud Parsons, *one of Chem-Labs' long-time supervisors, nods his support and says,* "I think you're right, Helen."

"We should reply to the Chinese immediately," Helen proposes. "Tell them we can still work out the deal. Ask them for more information. Let's draft a fax back to them."

"Why don't we try to set up a meeting," Bud suggests. "Someone should go over there," *he states, looking at Helen.*

"That's a good idea, Bud," Helen replies. "Personal relationships mean a lot to the Chinese. I am willing to work on setting that up."

"Just hold on," Barry says in a raised voice. "We should wait to see about Tom's condition. It will be risky to move ahead. I say we wait.

Let's keep our energies focused on domestic operations for now. They offer more certainty than the China venture. We don't want to do anything rash." Barry *looks directly at Helen.* "No one here was directly involved in the negotiations with the Chinese. I say we wait."

Roger Klein, another of the company's managers, shrugs in apparent resignation. "Barry's in charge," *he concedes.* "We should comply with what Barry says."

"Look," Helen *responds, her eyes narrowing,* "I know how the project unfolded. I say we can keep it going."

"Come on, Helen," Roger *says,* "you're new to the firm—"

Helen *cuts him off and speaks with emphasis.* "Roger, I know how much potential this deal holds for us. We should keep working on it."

Tony Franzini, another manager, looks toward Barry and says, "I agree with Helen. We should give her idea a try." *He then turns to Helen.* "Do you think the fax really means they want to pull out?"

"That's a good question," Helen *replies.* "My experience is they rely on hidden messages. It's part of their cautious approach to strangers. Tom is the only one who has met them face-to-face. They sized him up and liked him, but they don't know any of us. So we need to initiate contact, develop a relationship with them."

Bud nods in agreement. He knows that Helen was brought into the company because of her experience in the Pacific Rim. "What approach should we take, Helen? How do we proceed?"

"It all depends," she *says thoughtfully.* "Naturally we have to be alert. The fax might also be a negotiating ploy to gain some new advantage. Our Chinese friends might be relying on one of their maxims, 'When the enemy is thrown into disorder, crush him.' I say we suggest a meeting with them—the sooner the better. Their response will tell us something about the strategy they're using."

Roger turns to Helen and speaks sternly: "Helen, Barry told us we have to hold off. He's the senior manager now. Barry said that—"

Helen's face hardens as she jumps in and says, "Roger, I know how the Chinese think. I say we can pull this off."

Roger turns toward Barry. "Who does she think she is?" *he mutters.*

"Look Helen," Barry *responds,* "I'm the firm's negotiation expert, not you. And I've been with the firm longer than anybody. You're

outside your authority." He scans the faces of the other members of the group. "I order you all to hold tight."

Tony Franzini leans toward Barry. "Barry, can't you see the logic? Helen's approach gives us an option. I support her."

Barry retorts, "I say we have to wait. We have to regroup. The important thing is—"

Helen interrupts and speaks to the entire group: "Holding back could kill the China deal. Our schedule calls for action within two days. If we take steps now, we might still pull it off. We've invested a lot in the China venture. We should move forward. It's a chance. It's something to try."

Barry looks around the room. "Don't listen to her!" he spits out. "I say we hold off!"

One of the supervisors murmurs, "Well, Barry's in charge." One of the senior-level employees states, "Yeah, we have to do what he says, don't we?" Several other employees nod.

Bud tries to counter these comments. "Helen's idea is a good one. We should set up the meeting. I'm willing to support her." Another supervisor says, "Okay, me too," and then two employees state in unison, "We're behind Helen."

When I ask members of both private and public organizations, "Who is the leader in this story?" almost everyone picks Helen Gitler. I agree. However, when I ask them what *makes* her the leader, the responses I get indicate a problem in the way people think about leadership.

People typically choose Helen because they perceive her as:

- Decisive
- The one with a vision
- Positive and enthusiastic
- Self-confident
- Willing to listen
- Interested in learning
- The one with expertise, credibility
- Action-oriented
- Encouraging to others

These are admirable qualities and behaviors. However, are they valid reasons for labeling Helen the leader in this story? Do they really explain what it *means* to be a leader?

Consider Barry Sherman. His actions and attributes are actually very similar to Helen's. Barry also has a "vision"—focus on domestic operations—and he is very decisive about the action the company should take. He, too, appears positive and confident about his view. Yet very few select him as the leader.

On the other hand, Barry tries to shut Helen out, which suggests he is a poor listener. However, Helen is an equally selective listener. She interrupts Barry and responds curtly to Roger Klein. Barry can also be criticized because he did not appear receptive to learning. Yet Helen did not display any interest in learning more about Barry's position either. Helen, it appears, does not consistently display some of the "leadership" qualities people ascribe to her.

Consider expertise. Helen's expertise about Chinese culture is used to explain her leadership abilities. Yet can't Barry be said to have more expertise, since he has longer tenure with the organization? Furthermore, he is the company's negotiation specialist, which gives him important credibility when it comes to guiding the organization in this chaotic situation.

The most frequently mentioned difference between Helen and Barry is that she is action-oriented while Barry advocates waiting. Suppose for the sake of discussion that Helen's action results in disaster. Imagine that following her advice causes even greater chaos, upsetting the organization's already unbalanced equilibrium. Furthermore, suppose that Barry's "action" (deciding to wait is a type of action) turns out to help the company dramatically. In such a scenario, Barry would be the hero and Helen the goat.

My point in making this last distinction is that the common "bias for action" label associated with leadership is actually a bias for successful action. Unfortunately, the outcome of any action is never completely certain. Attributing leadership to those with an "action-orientation" does not seem to be a completely valid descriptor of a leader.

I am, of course, playing devil's advocate regarding this story and the labels used to describe its two main characters. I *do* believe that Helen was a leader, and I *do not* believe that Barry is. I will return to a discussion of Helen and Barry in Chapter 2 and offer my explanation of their roles in this story. My real purpose in comparing Helen and Barry is to demonstrate that what makes Helen a leader is *not*, essentially, a function of the qualities and behaviors people usually ascribe to her.

Critical Questions

What, then, makes Helen, or anyone else, a leader? What is leadership? When and how does leadership occur? And what enables some people to become leaders?

Answers to these questions are central to understanding leadership and to describing how to lead. Today's competitive realities make those answers more important than ever. Rapid, accelerating, unrelenting change has altered the foundation of corporate enterprise and government bureaucracy. Organizations and government agencies are under tremendous pressure since they have been RRRECQD (pronounced "wrecked"). That is, *r*einventing, *r*ightsizing, *r*eengineering, *e*mpowerment, *c*ustomer- and *q*uality-*d*riven efforts have transformed the way they operate. More and better leaders are essential to guide organizations in today's changing, unpredictable environment.

Efforts to understand leaders and leadership have not been completely satisfactory. The shelves of local bookstores and libraries bulge with thousands of leadership texts, almost every one of them providing a different model or theory. Unfortunately, many leadership models contradict each other, and none has achieved universal acceptance among those who aspire to lead.

While we have learned a lot, the most fundamental order, patterns, and practices that define leadership and how to lead are still not clearly defined, and no integrated explanation has been provided. To fulfill the search for leadership requires defining the "natural laws" of leadership.

2

The Nine Natural Laws
of Leadership

"I ask, how would nature solve this? I try to think like nature to find the right questions. You don't invent the answers, you reveal the answers from nature. In nature the answers to our problems already exist."

—Dr. Jonas Salk, inventor of Salk vaccine

If you could simultaneously view all of the interactions within your organization, you would notice obvious patterns, and many of these patterns would be predictably consistent, occurring in the same way day after day. People arrive and leave work; they hold meetings and communicate; they produce products and provide services in recognizably repeatable ways. Some patterns occur less frequently, but they are never the less fairly stable.

Patterns of Nature

The regular patterns in any discipline represent the "laws of nature" for that field. Natural law describes the intelligence or order that occurs in the universe. The motion of the planets, the

7

growth of plants, the structure of DNA, and nature's most primary transformations—of matter into energy and energy back into matter—occur because of laws that govern the action and direction of these processes.

The definable patterns of human interaction that occur in organizations represent *their* laws of nature. Understanding those laws and being able to operate in accordance with them provides greater individual and organizational effectiveness.

Of course, not all organizational activity fits into predictable formations. Some events appear chaotic. Irregularity and unpredictability infect organization life. New competitive opportunities create uncertainty. Small changes in certain conditions can trigger wild fluctuations in activity. One person leaves a group, and suddenly the group cannot function effectively. Two individuals engage in a battle of wills, and an entire organization rages in destructive conflict. A technological breakthrough opens up a lucrative market niche. A change in trade laws creates new possibilities for unlimited commerce.

The locus of leadership lies in the randomness, uncertainty, and opportunity inherent in these situations. Leaders provide direction and guidance through chaos and they take advantage of unchartered opportunities. Leaders help entire organizations grapple with competitive survival and pursue strategies into unknown arenas. Leaders become important when divisions or individual departments struggle to be effective and pursue dramatic improvements. Even localized irregularities, such as a work group gone off track or a team focused on meeting a new product quality initiative, require a leader.

The Elusive Mystery: The Leadership Pattern

The complexity inherent in leadership has created difficulty in defining it and in describing how to lead effectively. A recognizable leadership pattern remains elusive because of the vast variety of leaders.

Consider the differences between several well known leaders: the compassion of Lincoln and the coldness of Lenin, for example, or the lofty and poetic rhetoric of Martin Luther King and the folksy analogies of Ross Perot. Picture the supportive, cheerleading approach of Mary Kay Ash, founder of Mary Kay Cosmetics, and then view the highly successful Linda Wachner, head of Warnaco clothiers, whom *Fortune* magazine described as tongue lashing, impatient, and one of America's "toughest bosses."

Leadership practice appears even messier because of its paradoxical reality. The same leadership approach can work in very different contexts, but a leadership strategy that works in one particular situation may not work again at another time under the same conditions.

Exploring Leadership's Deeper Realities

Science resolves nature's mysteries by delving into its primary patterns. The most fundamental natural laws exist as intelligence waiting to be discovered. For example, as late as the 1920s, even Nobel Prize winners in physics firmly held that the atom was indivisible. More fundamental natural laws describe the primary sources of nature's energy and creativity. Further investigation revealed deeper truths that allowed us to split the atom. The atom is more fundamental and has greater power than the molecule, and the subatomic level is more basic and powerful than the atomic tier.

To understand and gain mastery of leadership requires uncovering its most fundamental natural laws. Such laws are valuable if they meet four criteria:

1. They precisely define what it means to be a leader across the complexity and range of leadership in all contexts. The pattern represented by the laws would apply as much to a single leader and follower as to a leader of a nation.

2. They clearly differentiate leaders from non-leaders and other organizational roles.
3. They effectively identify the common source of all leadership capability.
4. They suggest practical action ideas that provide useful choices for those who take the lead in their organizations.

The nine natural laws of leadership that I posit all meet these four standards. These laws draw from the most compelling insights of many thoughtful practitioners and scholars, and they offer a new focus regarding the meaning and practice of leadership. They build on and reinforce each other to provide an integrated portrait of leadership. Each one suggests practical actions—which I call action ideas—that leaders can use to align themselves with each of the nine laws and increase their leadership power. The action ideas do not represent absolute "right" or guaranteed ways to predict a specific result in a particular circumstance; rather they represent choices for the artful application of leadership.

The Nine Natural Laws of Leadership

The nine natural laws of leadership are as follows:

1. A leader has willing followers-allies.
2. "Leadership" is a field of interaction—a relationship between leaders and followers-allies.
3. Leadership occurs as an event.
4. Leaders use influence beyond formal authority.
5. Leaders operate outside the boundaries of organizationally defined procedures.
6. Leadership involves risk and uncertainty.
7. Not everyone will follow a leader's initiative.
8. Consciousness — information processing capacity— creates leadership.

9. Leadership is a self-referral process. Leaders and followers process information from their own subjective, internal frame of reference.

Natural Law 1: A Leader Has Willing Followers

What does it mean to be a leader? The first natural law of leadership answers this fundamental question: A leader has willing followers. No leader exists without gaining the support of others. Yet this core element of what it means to be a leader is typically overlooked.

The traditional view defines leaders by a list of traits, qualities, habits, or behaviors. However, as the comparison between Helen and Barry outlined in Chapter 1 shows, individual qualities and behaviors do *not* clearly differentiate leaders from nonleaders. Helen and Barry display similar attributes, yet Helen is the leader because Bud, Tony, and others willingly follow her direction. She has their commitment. Those who go along with Barry comply only because he "is in charge" and is the "one with authority." They *have to* listen to him.

Followers are the underlying element that defines all leaders in all situations. The well-known individuals noted above—Lincoln, Lenin, King, Perot, Ash, and Wachner—were leaders when they gained followers.

Typically all glory and grandeur goes to the leader, and being a follower is usually thought of as a second-class or low-status role. The first natural law of leadership changes our view of followers because it recognizes the collegial, partnering role they play. Followers are allies who represent the necessary opposite side of the leadership coin.

Understanding the follower as a necessary ally is central to explain the complexity of leading. In 1993, both Gerald Levin and N. J. "Nick" Nicholas sought to lead Time-Warner, the company Steve Ross created by merging the publishing and film production companies. Levin prevailed because he had the willing support of Ross and the company's board of directors. Nicholas was an accomplished executive with talent, drive, a good track

record, and many other fine qualities, but he could not get the
key players at Time-Warner to follow or align themselves with
him. In the bid to guide Time-Warner, he was not a leader. Gaining and keeping followers-allies is the leader's basic requirement.

> *Action Idea: Focus on gaining followers.* When you choose
> to take initiative on a particular task, ask yourself, "Who do
> I need to follow or align themselves with me?" or "Whose
> support is necessary?" Then concentrate on gaining the
> backing of these people.

Natural Law 2: Leadership Is a Field of Interaction—A Relationship Between Leaders and Followers.

Leaders and leadership are not the same. When people say, "We
need better leadership," they typically mean, "We need a different leader." However, "leadership" represents something more
than the leader alone; it encompasses the leader and the follower
together.

The second natural law of leadership thus explains that the
power we call leadership refers to the *interaction* of leader and
follower. Followers are allies who join the leader, and together
they create the energy that drives organizations. In Chapter 1,
Helen's leadership occurred when Bud, Tony, and others
aligned with her proposed direction.

The mistaken idea that leadership power resides within a
single person most frequently occurs in the case of heroic, highly
visible leaders. Consider how Lee Iacocca is credited with the
dramatic turnaround of Chrysler, how Steve Jobs is acclaimed as
the creator of Apple Computer, or how Gloria Steinem is hailed
for the emergence of the women's movement. Yet all three had
impact only in relationship with their followers.

Leadership is not a person, a position, or a program but a
relationship or field of interaction that occurs when the leader
and the follower connect. The leadership field is an undivided
wholeness that resembles a dance. Watch Fred Astaire and Gin-

ger Rogers dance in one of their exquisite routines. The symmetry of the dance does not unfold from Fred's graceful lead alone, from Ginger's flawless following, or from the dance's spellbinding choreography. The wonder of the dance emanates from the totality of Fred-Ginger-music-movement-floor. The dance is a *field*—a pattern of relationship that connects all the diverse parts simultaneously.

Leadership is also a dance, the interacting ebb and flow between leader and follower. To understand the leadership field we must, as Gary Zukav advised in *The Dancing Wu Li Masters* regarding all of nature, "observe the dance." Pay attention to the interaction between leader and follower, and consider their relationship.

> *Action Idea: Build solid work relationships with others.* The quality of relationships you have with others is central to leadership. Others are more likely to follow when you step forward to lead if they know you and trust you. Building solid work relationships is an ongoing activity.

Natural Law 3: Leadership Occurs as an Event

People usually view leadership as continuous—an ongoing characteristic of a great person and a set of enduring habits, values, or standards. The common phrase *natural-born leader* reinforces the belief that leadership is a durable quality. This approach fails to appreciate that leadership exists as the leader-follower field and that these alliances are transitory.

Anyone who has struggled with the challenge of leading knows how tenuous it can be. People can lose interest in a leader's particular path. In the early 1990s, the General Motors board deposed Robert Stempel because they felt he could not steer the organization onto the right track. In 1992, Americans abandoned George Bush because they wanted change. Leaders also know that their initiatives require capturing, and then recapturing, followers' commitment. Bill Clinton's 1992 election as America's leader was followed by a repeated struggle to maintain support for his legislative efforts.

The third natural law of leadership reveals that leadership occurs as an event. Leader-follower fields begin, have a middle, and they end. They occur as discrete interactions each time a leader and follower join. Helen's leadership event as described in Chapter 1 originated when Bud followed her suggestion to contact the Chinese. That specific event enlarged when Helen gained Tony as a follower, and it expanded again when one of the supervisors and two of the employees joined with her. Her leadership event will exist as long as others follow Helen's lead for this particular venture.

Leadership can appear continuous if a leader manifests multiple leadership events. Some followers remain loyal to a particular leader over long periods of time and support that leader throughout a variety of circumstances. For example, Margaret Thatcher maintained a core of willing followers throughout her twelve-year tenure as British prime minister. Her leadership ended in 1992 when John Majors gained a greater number of followers. The bulk of leadership events, however, have a shorter shelf-life. They occur as brief leader-follower interactions in specific circumstances. Gaps exist between gaining followers in one circumstance and attracting them or others in another situation.

The concept of leadership as an event explains that leadership occurs throughout organizations, with numerous leaders gaining followers in a variety of situations. In small group meetings that get off track, a leadership event occurs when someone gains support to redirect the group on its agenda. A leadership event happens when one person offers direction that another willingly accepts, or when someone inspires an entire organization or community to support a particular direction. When people gain followers up or down the corporate and governmental ladder, energy surges in the organization as discrete events of leadership power.

Action Idea: Concentrate on the leadership event. Accept the variable duration and scope of your ability to gain followers. Take initiative when action is needed to gain followers-allies. Create the field when necessary. Share leadership power by reinforcing others as willing followers-allies.

Natural Law 4: Leaders Use Influence Beyond Formal Authority

Leaders gain followers through influence; however, managers also rely on influence to get things done. The difference between the two is the source of the leader's influence. Consider how Helen influenced Bud and Tony to follow in Chapter 1. Helen did not force Bud to join her, and she had no formal authority over Tony since they were peers in the organizational hierarchy. Bud and Tony willingly committed to her because of her ideas and her experience. In contrast, those who supported Barry clarified that his influence was based on his being "in charge."

A common belief is that being the boss makes a person a leader, yet managerial influence and leadership influence are quite different. A leader's influence arises from followers' interactions with him or her, while a manager's influence stems from the manager's position in the hierarchy. Leadership is person-to-person influence; management is position-to-position (superior to subordinate) influence. Management authority is defined by the rigid lines on the organizational chart; leadership influence occurs as a spider web of interactions that link people who want to join together. Leader-follower interactions are based on commitment; manager-subordinate associations rely on command. The leader inspires others to want to follow or align with him or her; a manager requires others to comply with organizationally defined demands that the manager has formal authority to rule.

Of course, managers can also wear the leader's belt. Helen was a manager, but those who supported her were not obeying her formal role; her followers willingly responded rather than merely submitted to a boss's directives. Furthermore, when gaining followers includes selection to a managerial position, a leader acquires managerial clout.

Action Idea: Develop influence beyond authority. Take on tasks relevant to the organization's core mission. Gain access to critical information networks (knowledge is power) and mentor other people; develop task expertise, attend training or formal education programs, and support others' work projects. All of these actions will increase your ability to influence people.

Natural Law 5: Leaders Operate Outside the Boundaries of Organizationally Defined Procedures

Leaders gain followers because people and organizations need direction. Although managers also provide direction, leaders chart direction in a different domain. In Chapter 1, both Barry and Helen outlined a path of action for their company. Barry's approach, to "stay the course," represented action within the established, organizationally defined plan. His course might be the right action, but his direction represents traveling along the established, structured track already laid down by the organization. Helen pointed in a direction beyond that prescribed by existing procedures. She stepped forth into unstructured territory.

The fifth natural law clarifies that leaders operate outside the prescribed lines created by organizational rules, regulations, policies, and procedures. A *leadership arena* exists when the institutional structure does not offer certain guidance on how to proceed.

Eventually in every organization, the established path becomes blocked, or people get stuck in a rut, or a new possibility exists that is not on the existing course. The leader steps up when no defined path exists. In the late 1980s, Barry Gibbons turned a loser into a winner by boosting Burger King's operating earnings 25 percent in the last fiscal quarter of 1989 over the year before. When Gibbons saw an opportunity in a new broiled-chicken sandwich, he introduced the product without the sacrosanct eighteen months of market testing, and over protests from the marketing department. Gibbons' willingness to step into a nonprescribed arena paid off, says Brian Dumaine in *Fortune*

(July 16, 1990): Burger King now sells 1 million broiled-chicken sandwiches a day.

A popular idea today is that "managers do things right" and "leaders do the right things." It is a catchy distinction. But how do we know the right thing except in retrospect? In 1993, IBM dumped John Akers and handed Lou Gerstner the helm. IBM insiders chose Gerstner because they felt he could succeed. But how can anyone prescribe the elusive "right thing" Gerstner must do to lead IBM?

Both leaders and managers do the right thing, and both have to do things right; they simply operate in different domains. The fifth natural law reveals that leaders emerge when people and organizations face unknown arenas that require someone to step up, take the lead, and gain willing followers-allies.

As Sun Tzu said in *The Art of War*, "Don't follow where the pathway goes, lead instead where there is no path and leave a trail."

Action Idea: Fix your sights on nonprescribed areas. Look for opportunities and seek ways to resolve problems beyond your job description and outside the prescribed organizational boundaries set by rules, regulations, policies, and procedures. Pay attention to projects or responsibilities that are not fully defined and have few established requirements. Focus on what is not working. Ask questions to identify possibilities and challenge assumptions. Ask yourself each day: "What more can I do to move the organization forward?"

Natural Law 6: Leadership Involves Risk and Uncertainty

Leaders live without a safety net. The unchartered leadership arena is fraught with ambiguity and chaos, and the leader's task always involves risk and uncertainty. Operating in the nonprescribed, unstructured leadership arena demands performing action in unstable circumstances. In Chapter 1, Barry sought to avoid risk; Helen was willing to embrace it.

The practical reality of leading requires accepting that risk and uncertainty are part of the leadership territory. Taking risks may not result in success because no one can completely control the results of action, and leaders recognize that they cannot ensure specific results. They nevertheless accept risk as part of the challenge of leading.

> *Action Idea: Embrace risk and uncertainty as a challenge.* Risk is an interpretation. View risk as a challenge, just as you might be energized to solve a knotty mathematical problem, succeed in a difficult negotiation, or perform well in a tough tennis match. Transform the tension created by uncertainty into the productive energy needed to take action. Use the adrenaline that typically flows during risky times as power that transforms anxiety into action. Then enjoy the action without being attached to the unpredictable fruits of action.

Natural Law 7: Not Everyone Will Follow a Leader's Initiative

Leaders face limits. Perhaps the most critical limit is that not everyone will follow a leader. In the late 1940s, W. Edwards Deming recognized the need for a new approach to manufacturing, but no one in America was interested in his ideas at that time. In the 1960s, the heads of IBM rejected Ross Perot's suggestion that IBM should service the software it sold. No leader, not even the so-called great leaders, such as Ghandi or Lincoln, has everyone's support.

Gaining followers is unpredictable. Allies can be hard to come by; some people reject the leader's initiative, and others stall when the leader suggests a course of action. In Chapter 1, Helen did not have the support of all the people in the meeting.

Efforts to prescribe a "correct" leadership style and directives that attempt to ensure leader effectiveness have limited utility. No one has a crystal ball to foretell the future. Uncertainty is always present, especially in the uncharted leadership arena. Some people do not trust that a leader can guide them effectively; others will not step into the risk-filled arena with anyone. To succeed requires focusing on those who will follow, gaining their support, and then moving forward.

> *Action Idea: Attend to those who will follow.* Since not everyone will always follow, focus on those who *will* support your lead. Pay attention to those who acknowledge your lead as useful, and give consideration to anyone who offers you positive support. Align with the critical followers by asking yourself, "Who must I get to follow me to achieve this initiative?" A few key allies can bring success to your initiative. Seek them out, but remember that sometimes no one will follow. The reasons are explained in the final two leadership laws.

Natural Law 8: Consciousness—Information Processing Capacity—Creates Leadership

Leadership begins with an idea that might resolve a problem or exploit an opportunity. A leader gains followers when he or she performs action that influences followers so they accept the leader's direction. In effect, the two become of one mind. Consciousness—the capacity to process information—is the underlying source of leadership power. The leadership dance occurs in the theater of consciousness.

Consciousness defines how people interpret information and create meaning from it. Through consciousness, leaders turn what Margaret Wheatley, in *Leadership and the New Science,* calls the environment's raw "information-energy" into a useful direction. Leaders gain followers-allies when both parties process information in similar ways. The mechanics of the process begin within the leader.

The leader's consciousness interacts with the nonprescribed, uncharted leadership arena. Leaders perceive opportunities and recognize how to overcome obstacles that others do not or cannot perceive. For example, in 1977 Larry Ellison, CEO and cofounder of the software company Oracle, was intrigued by an IBM research publication on relational database management that allowed users to analyze information in any way they wanted rather than along rigidly defined, predetermined lines. Recognizing the boon provided by this flexibility, Ellison and Oracle cofounder Bob Miner wrote and marketed a relational database program three years ahead of IBM. Ellison also adapted the Oracle version to run on mainframes and smaller computers made by any manufacturer, while IBM's version ran only on its more costly equipment. Oracle became an attractive alternative for those seeking lower-cost data management. By 1994, Oracle had $1.6 billion in annual sales, making it the top corporate database producer, and Oracle held a 34 percent to 26 percent market share edge over IBM, reports Alan Deutschman in *Fortune* (November 29, 1993).

Simply stated, leaders think differently from others. Leaders have the ability to integrate information that is sometimes unrelated into new, more useful wholes that offer solutions and provide direction. In Chapter 1, Helen interpreted her company's chaotic situation as a time to move ahead. Barry processed information in terms of the prescribed boundaries of the organization's existing course of action. His direction gave expression to a path already defined by the organization. His idea was not wrong; rather, it did not represent a leader's path: an insight into the nonprescribed leadership arena.

A leader must influence followers to recognize his or her direction as useful. Leaders connect with followers when followers go "on-line" with the leader's level of consciousness. Helen's interpretation resonated with Tony and Bud, so they supported her lead; their consciousness moved with hers. The leader-follower field is a bond or interaction of consciousness. The shared field represents collective consciousness in action, united by an idea about how to solve a problem or exploit a possibility.

A November 1994 *Fortune* magazine article by Kenneth Labich identified the most common reasons companies fail. Underlying Labich's conclusions is that companies blunder because of the limited consciousness of those who should be providing direction. Companies fail because people do not effectively process information regarding the fundamentals of an industry or business—managers do not understand key profitability drivers. People do not ask key questions about an organization's core expertise—managers are clueless about what made their organizations successful in the first place. People do not perceive and overcome potential obstacles—managers suffer from short attention spans. People rely on established premises that do not match current reality—managers cannot see the need to move beyond what worked in the past. And organizations fail because people do not understand their most important customer needs, nor do they understand why their customers defect to competitors—managers fail to install a formal system for distilling and interpreting information from the field.

Sears, once America's retail giant, fell far behind Wal-Mart in the early 1990s. Sears stumbled because its managers ignored signals from its environment. Well into the 1980s, Sears's competitive strategic analyses did not even include mention of Wal-Mart as a competitive threat despite Wal-Mart's huge success. The unwillingness or inability to process that information strangled Sears's market competitiveness.

Leaders also misfire when they cannot change their followers' consciousness and gain their commitment to the leader's direction. The leader's power, influence beyond authority, occurs on the level of consciousness. In the early 1990s, John Akers was deposed as head of IBM. He could not convince others that the solution to Big Blue's problems was to break it up into several "Baby Blues." IBM's board of directors did not buy it. The breakup plan was scrapped soon after Akers was replaced. Akers could not enlighten the board to his way of thinking, and they pushed Akers aside.

In a larger sense, leaders either shape the followers' consciousness or leaders can do no more than mirror the people's consciousness. Typically we view leaders in the driver's seat, steering their organizations with a sure and steady hand. But leaders can attract only followers who are on a similar wavelength of awareness. Leaders must meet the follower at the follower's level of consciousness before they can lead the follower to a new level.

The leader as shaper and mirror of consciousness clarifies the paradoxes inherent in leadership. People want leaders to guide them forward toward new and better results, but they also expect leaders to take them where the people want to go. People look to leaders for direction, but are unwilling to follow leaders unless they meet the people's needs. In essence, leaders attempt to stretch people beyond boundaries so they step into the nonprescribed leadership arena, but leaders must also calibrate their actions to fit the people's consciousness. In the final analysis, leaders reflect the followers, and followers get the leaders they deserve.

The failure to address the role of consciousness in leadership is perhaps the most glaring weakness in existing leadership theory and prescription. Typically books on leadership explore only the outward manifestation of consciousness, such as the actions and the attributes the leader displays. Only a few include a discussion of consciousness or even a reference to consciousness. Among these books are Peter Vaill's *Managing as a Performing Art*, Peter Senge's *The Fifth Discipline*, and Margaret Wheatley's *Leadership and the New Science*; and in J. Renesch's edited collection, *New Traditions in Business*, the chapter by Michael Ray explains the importance of consciousness to reality. A full understanding of leadership requires awareness of how information processing creates the leadership field.

Action Idea: Develop greater self-awareness. Greater self-awareness means knowing the strengths and limitations of your consciousness. Become aware of how you restrict or overload your information reception process. Explore the assumptions and judgments you make when you interpret information. Are your assumptions based on information or derived from what you suppose exists? Do your judgments represent old mental programs, or are they formed through a dialectic learning process of thesis-antithesis-synthesis? Think about how you respond to information. Are you overly cautious and unwilling to commit to action; do you move to the other extreme and act without thinking; or do you balance analytical with intuitive analysis? Continually update your information base. Explore alternate ways to interpret data. Use different models to evaluate ideas.

Natural Law 9: Leadership Is a Self-Referral Process

Leaders and followers process information from their own subjective, internal frame of reference. Consciousness is *how* people process information. Self-referral defines *who* processes the information.

Knowledge, intelligence, experience, judgment, and wisdom are structured in the subjective state of one's consciousness, just as the structure of a computer software program defines how it processes information. But human consciousness transcends computing; it is knowing you are computing. The "knower" is the self, the inner identity who does the computing; the "self" that processes information determines reality.

Self-referral explains that the world is as we are, based on our subjective state of consciousness. Leaders interpret and respond to problems and possibilities in a manner consistent with their states of consciousness. For example, consider the differences in the massive social programs of Lyndon Baines Johnson's Great Society and Ronald Reagan's anti–big government agenda. Compare the nonviolence of Ghandi with the cruelty of Hitler. And recall Susan B. Anthony's fight for women's voting rights versus turn-of-the-century President Grover Cleveland's statement, "Sensible and responsible women do not want to vote." Every leader sees the world through his or her specific lenses. Similarly, followers identify with the leader because the leader fits the followers' self-referral image of what a leader should be. The followers accept the leader's course of action because they have self-referral with the direction.

In Chapter 1, Helen had self-referral with the China venture. Her inner self, the structure of her subjective consciousness, interpreted the situation in a way that urged her to take action to maintain the deal. When Bud stated, "I think you're right, Helen," and Tony remarked, "I agree with Helen," they demonstrated their self-referral with Helen and her ideas. From their level of consciousness, Helen made sense. Barry, in contrast, had little self-referral with the China operation. He could not identify with Helen or with her direction. When challenged by Tony, Barry could not "see the logic" behind Helen's idea.

Leaders fail to gain followers when they do not meet the followers at their level of consciousness. For example, a manager for a wholesale food distributor proposed several customer service and team development efforts to improve her work group's lagging effectiveness. Members of the group commented, "This isn't of any value to us," "The problem lies elsewhere," and "She doesn't understand what's going on." The manager had not established the connection with their level of consciousness that was necessary for her to influence them to follow.

The self-referral concept is central to understanding and practicing leadership. Most leadership models attempt to define objective determinants to describe leaders; they imply that leadership exists as an entity separate from the leader and the followers' subjective point of view. Self-referral clarifies that leadership exists within—in the consciousness of the leader and the followers.

Self-referral also explains why divisive and destructive leadership fields occur. Some leaders function from a less evolved, restricted, or even violent state of consciousness. The horrors wrought by Adolph Hitler, Joseph Stalin, Jim Jones, and David Koresh reveal their self-referral interpretation of reality. Followers who support destructive leaders operate from a similar state of consciousness. Negative fields of collective consciousness exist because of a narrowly defined self, a self-referral identity structured in terms of harmful beliefs, values, and judgments.

Self-referral reveals the first and foremost directive to develop leadership power. Leaders have to expand their consciousness so they operate from a more unified, enlightened state. Leaders must transcend the boundaries that limit or prejudicially distort perception. The expansion of consciousness shifts leaders from seeing themselves in the world to seeing the world in themselves.

> *Action Idea: Clarify expectations.* Expectations reveal one filter people use to interpret reality. What we expect is what we get. To lead requires continually exploring what matters to others, how they interpret events, and the meaning they assign to a situation. To discover the self-referral identity people use to define their world, hold meetings in which expectations are clarified. Ask participants, "What do you expect from . . . ?" "What is important to you about . . . ?" The answers will help you meet the followers at their level of consciousness.
>
> Clarify your expectations to make it easier for others to understand and accept your position. The potential to manifest the leadership field increases when leaders and followers understand each other's self-referral frame of reference.

* * *

The laws of nature are not necessarily benevolent; hurricanes, floods, earthquakes, and disease are part of natural law, and they can be destructive. Similarly, the nine natural laws describe both life-supporting leaders and destructive ones. To realize benefit from aligning with and mastering the natural laws of leadership requires creating more and better life-supporting leaders and limiting the emergence of harmful leaders. The nine natural laws of leadership provide a means to achieve this end because they are based on a paradigm that allows us to prescribe more enlightened leadership practice.

3

The Quantum Leadership Paradigm

"A paradigm shift is like a boat, you don't want to miss it."
—*John Huey,* Fortune *magazine writer*

I boarded the plane at Washington National Airport, took a book out of my briefcase, and began to read. The woman in the seat next to me glanced at the book and asked, "Are you a physicist?"

"No," I answered.

"But that's a physics book, isn't it?" she persisted.

"Yes," I began to explain, but she immediately broke in, "Do you work in an R&D lab?"

"No," I replied.

"Then you must be helping one of your kids with a science project," she said.

I paused for a moment to get her attention and said, "Actually, I provide leadership consulting and training programs. I'm reading this book to help me understand the laws of leadership."

Her inquisitive expression turned into a puzzled look. "What," she asked incredulously, "does physics have to do with leadership?"

The Physics of Leadership

Most people do not recognize a connection between leadership and physics, which they view as far removed from the challenges and demands of organizational life. Although stories of leaders—both the heroes who satisfy and the villains who disappoint—fascinate us, images of atoms and Einstein often just bewilder us.

Yet leadership and physics share a common focus. Physics explains the energy, matter, and motion that define how the universe works. In the same way, leadership is the power that galvanizes human energy and translates it into action. So the exercise of leadership can be viewed as the practice of human physics.

Leadership today is understood in terms of the seventeenth-century paradigm developed by Sir Isaac Newton known as classical physics—a set of laws that defined what were proposed as the "ironclad laws of nature." Newton's paradigm, revolutionary for its time, was supposed to describe the final and complete model of the universe. More recent investigations into natural law, however, have shown that the classical physics paradigm offers only a partial view of nature's order.

At the beginning of the twentieth century, a new paradigm, known as quantum physics, revealed a more fundamental reality of nature and in the process shattered the idea that the Newtonian worldview was the final word on natural law: Quantum physics revealed a more primary power and order of nature, and explained events that were beyond the scope of Newton's paradigm. Classical physics still offers a "correct" view of certain aspects of nature, but quantum physics describes deeper layers of natural law.

The assumptions that define Newton's paradigm of reality are the basis for most descriptions of leadership. Furthermore, the classical physics assumptions have limited a full and complete understanding of leadership. Quantum physics is based on a set of assumptions that provide a platform to explain the meaning of leadership more clearly and to more effectively describe how to lead. A shift to a quantum view of leadership also offers a way to develop more life-supporting, enlightened leadership.

The Shift to Quantum Leadership

Toward the end of our flight, my inquisitive seatmate again asked if she really had to understand physics to grasp the full meaning of leadership. I explained that from one point of view, she did not: She did not have to understand the force of gravity in order to avoid spinning off the planet. And she did not need to know more clearly about DNA in order to get to work each day. Yet I also explained that by understanding the basic assumptions of physics that underlie our view of leadership, she would have a clearer insight into the leader's complex task. By embracing a quantum view, I said, people can harness more leadership power and direct that power in more positive directions.

The nine natural laws of leadership are based on the quantum physics paradigm assumptions. They reveal that leadership is better understood and practiced as a quantum phenomenon. The nine laws provide a new view of leadership, the Quantum Leadership paradigm, which expands the potentiality for constructive leadership.

Two Views of Leadership

The Quantum Leadership paradigm differs from the classical physics view in terms of five critical assumptions, as shown in the table on the next page.

The Quantum Paradigm provides a language and a framework for more clearly understanding and more fully describing leadership practice than the approach offered through Newton's worldview. The rest of this chapter presents the Quantum Leadership paradigm by describing these five sets of assumptions

Classical Physics View of Leadership	Quantum Physics View of Leadership
1. Leadership is its parts.	1. Leadership is a field.
2. Leadership is a continuous attribute of a person.	2. Leadership is a discontinuous event.
3. Leadership influence is based on force.	3. Leadership influence is an interaction.
4. Leadership conforms to cause-and-effect logic.	4. Leadership is unstructured and unpredictable.
5. Leadership is an objective phenomenon.	5. Leadership is a subjective phenomenon.

and explains how the quantum view of leadership enables us to harness the full power of leadership and use that power in a more enlightened way.

Leadership Parts vs. the Leadership Field

Several years ago, a middle manager from a large petroleum company asked me if I had read Ken Follett's *On the Wings of Eagles,* a crackling account of the rescue in 1978 of two EDS executives from a heavily guarded fortress in Iran by a group of hand-picked EDS volunteers trained by a retired Green Beret lieutenant colonel. The petroleum manager reverently recounted Follett's description of Ross Perot, the head of EDS, and Perot's exceptional character traits: his boldness, his active response to crisis, and his strength of will. The manager then shook his head knowingly and proclaimed, "Now that's leadership!" His view reflected a widespread, but inaccurate, assumption about leadership derived from the classical physics paradigm. While I agreed that Perot's actions were admirable, I also explained that being a leader is *not* defined by an individual's attributes or behaviors.

Leadership Parts

The traditional assumption about leadership is that it can be explained by describing the parts: the habits, characteristics, and behaviors of single individuals. According to this perspective, leadership becomes the decisive force of GE's CEO Jack Welch, the intuitive genius of Microsoft's Bill Gates, the commanding presence of General Norman Schwarzkopf, or the compassionate patience of Mother Teresa.

This parts view stems from the impact of Newton's paradigm on our leadership mind-set. Newton described reality as made up of separate, solid bits of matter, which means that to understand reality, you must examine its distinct, visible building blocks. Through this lens, it makes sense to examine individual attributes or qualities of certain leaders and then develop lists of specific "leadership" traits or habits. Since the parts define Newtonian reality, leadership has become a composite of the qualities of leaders only, and "leadership" has become the singular centerpiece represented by a single individual. Yet this approach does not fit the fundamental reality that leaders do not exist without followers and that their individual characteristics or habits are relevant only as part of the leader-follower field of interaction.

The Leadership Field

Leadership is better understood as a field of interaction. It is not so much personal as it is interpersonal. Quantum physics asserts that to know nature, you must view it as a set of interconnected fields. At the deeper layers of natural law, no separate parts exist, and nothing that resembles visible, solid matter can be seen. The field is the fundamental reality, an undivided wholeness of information-energy. Through the quantum lens it appears that you are looking through a porthole that frames only the ocean, and you cannot distinguish any waves or droplets of water as separate and distinct from the ocean. You see only the homogeneous oneness of the field. As Danah Zohar explains in

The Quantum Self, the integral reality of a quantum field compares to the many voices of a choir that merge into one.

Through the quantum lens we recognize the leadership field. Those who initiate an action become leaders only when someone follows or becomes an ally *(the first natural law of leadership).* The leader's individual characteristics and behaviors have meaning only in relationship with followers-allies. Jack Welch transformed GE because of hard-nosed decisions such as massive employee layoffs and the sale of several of GE's business units, which earned him the label "neutron Jack." But this tough-mindedness was not what made him a leader. Rather, it was the people who followed him.

The field reality of leadership may seem abstract and distant from our ordinary experience. However, we now recognize the field reality of organizations. Walk into any organization and notice the pervasive "look and feel" of the place, the purposeful and ordered interactions between the workers and their tasks. You are witnessing an organization's culture—the nonmaterial, invisible field of shared beliefs and assumptions. The patterns of behavior, the physical layout, the artifacts on the walls, the configuration of materials on desks make up the culture's observable effect, but the company's culture, a nonmaterial field of regularities, underlies its surface appearance.

Quantum Leadership focuses attention on the interaction, not the separate parts, as the key to understanding leadership. A central interaction is the leader-follower relationship *(the second natural law of leadership).* Thus, "leadership" at Microsoft is not Bill Gates's innovativeness but the unity or connection between Gates and his people.

Field-conscious Quantum Leaders seek ways to draw the creative intelligence of individuals together, unit it, and increase the power to play out success in their organizations. Jesse Jackson offered a succinct description of the leadership field reality when he commented that leaders do not choose sides but rather bring sides together.

Field-conscious Quantum Leaders continually build bridges and establish common ground so that others become more receptive to their leadership initiatives. These leaders focus on the allies they need in specific circumstances—gaining support for a department-level project, acquiring commitment for a city-wide initiative, getting backing for an organization-wide re-structuring effort from key constituents, or securing sponsorship for a three-person committee. They then identify the necessary followers-allies and seek ways to draw them into a field of inter-action that aligns both parties in the same direction.

Ronald Reagan proved to be a master of this process. Upon assuming the presidency in 1980, he and his wife held intimate dinner parties in the White House, to which he invited members of Congress, the press, and various other powerful people. These dinners were not about politics or the global, national, or even local issues of the day. Reagan did not direct the table talk to economic, social, or political matters. Rather, he and Nancy Reagan told stories of their life together, charming their guests with intimate details about what they thought and how they felt. And the Reagans eagerly inquired about their guests, attended closely to their disclosures, and cheered and encouraged their stories. Reagan used these dinner parties to build a base of rela-tionships, labeled by some as "networking" and by others as "bonding." Quantum Leaders realize they must establish the mutual trust and confidence that enhances the possibility of gaining willing followers.

Failure to comprehend the importance of the field can de-stroy business opportunities. *Business Week* reported how in 1989, sales dropped at computer products dealer Businessland because founder and CEO David A. Norman tried to strong-arm Houston-based computer manufacturer Compaq. Norman wanted Compaq to match product discounts similar to those he had extracted from IBM, which were higher than those given to other retailers. Compaq balked and pulled its products from Businessland's shelves, dealing Norman's company a harsh blow, since Compaq accounted for 15 percent of Businessland's annual sales. According to a July 2, 1990, *Business Week* article, Norman failed to cultivate the complex interrelationship be-tween suppliers and resellers that are essential in his industry.

The field view expands leadership power. Quantum Leadership recognizes that the leader *and* the follower contribute to leadership. *Both* are necessary participants. Organizations that reward leaders *and* followers reinforce and expand the role both play in creating the power that drives organizations.

Quantum Leadership truly empowers people. A leader is empowered by recognizing that he or she influences the quality of interaction with followers. Willing followers are not second-class citizens. They are not passive like sheep who flock to the shepherd's call. Rather, they are empowered by recognizing how they fuel the leader's fire. Followers enable leaders by supporting the leader's initiative.

Thinking of leadership as a field provides everyone with a mind-set to respond effectively to the ever-increasing diversity within organizations. Quantum Leadership acknowledges that leaders cannot perceive themselves as separate from others. Rather than dismiss the diverse needs and interests of others, field-conscious leaders recognize the need to build a common ground to unite with needed followers.

Action Idea: Ask the right leadership questions. Most people who aspire to lead ask the wrong initial questions. "How do I lead?" or, "What do I have to do to be a leader?" reveal a mistaken belief that leadership is made up of parts. The correct questions are, "How do I get others to follow me?" "What are the needs of others?" and "How do I gain allies?"

Action Idea: Unmask "Lone Ranger leadership." "Lone Ranger leadership" reflects the assumption that leadership can be found in the habits and behaviors of one person. The fabled masked man was the sole author of law, order, and success. Personal sketches of bold and daring lone individuals and vivid descriptions of their style and flair fill leadership folklore. To clarify the reality of leadership as a field, unmask Lone Ranger leadership. Define leadership in your organization in terms of the field of leader-follower interaction. Each time someone claims that leadership is one person, challenge that assumption. Demonstrate how the leader and follower work together to create the power of leadership. Provide others with examples from specific work experiences showing that the focus on the leader alone masks leadership's essential reality. Clarify to others that leadership lies in the unity of leaders and followers.

Action Idea: Expand your field into different parts of the organization. Most of us interact with the same people each day based on the places we typically visit over the course of the workday. This is what I call personal traffic pattern (PTP). Sometimes the pattern becomes so fixed that we fail to realize we have limited our interactions with others. In fact, sometimes we shy away from certain work areas because we are unfamiliar with the people in them.

Alter and expand your PTP to establish better relationships with a wider network of people and to expand the scope of your interactions field. Spend time getting to know others in areas you typically do not visit. Expand your radar screen of awareness to tune in with people who work in areas related to your job. Patricia Grysavage, Director of Executive Management and Communications for the Department of Veterans Affairs, uses this action idea by spending fifteen minutes a week in areas of her organization she rarely visits. Joe Frick, Director of the Management Services Division in the U.S. Department of Agriculture, spends one day a month talking to employees in various divisions about important work efforts. Like Pat and Joe, seek ways to expand your field of interactions. Time spent in "new" areas will increase your capacity to establish leadership fields, since the foundation of relationship will be in place.

Leadership Continuity vs. Leadership Discontinuity

Consider the stories about several well-known individuals: Lee Iacocca led Chrysler out of debt; Gloria Steinem guided the modern women's movement to prominence; Steve Jobs harvested Apple into a golden business; Dwight D. Eisenhower directed the Normandy Invasion in World War II. Frances Hesselbein revitalized the Girl Scouts of America. I label these people "high-visibility media leaders" because of the frequent portrayals of their larger-than-life personas in news stories, books, and on television. Certainly these individuals deserve credit for their numerous, impactful leadership actions, but their stories fuel a mistaken belief about leadership as a continuous attribute or action.

Leadership as a Continuous Attribute

Viewing leadership as continuous reflects the impact of Newton's paradigm that perceives action as a seamless flow: When a ball rolls down a hill, you can observe the ball at every point. This continuous model describes the reality of solid matter quite well, but it fails to describe leadership. Some people gain followers only for a short time and only once in a while. Recall some recent meetings in your own organization. Can you remember how one person emerged to gain willing followers for a specific idea, then another person stepped forward to further that initiative or take a different tack, and then perhaps a third person took the lead? A meeting chairperson's position might remain continuous, but several different people often surface to take the lead. The leadership mantle frequently moves around the room as different leaders gain followers.

Thinking of leadership as a continuous attribute masks the reality that all leaders, even the so-called great ones, do not permanently maintain followers. Consider the roller-coaster leadership career of Lee Iacocca. Iacocca ascended to the presidency of Ford, was fired abruptly, and then reemerged to guide Chrysler successfully. Recall how Steve Jobs blossomed with Apple and then bombed with NeXT. Iacocca, Jobs, and all other prominent leaders have periods when they cannot continue to attract followers.

Leadership as a Discontinuous Event

Leadership is better understood as a discontinuous reality. Leaders and followers connect as an event *(the third natural law of leadership)* that can manifest itself over various time spans. Discontinuity is a quantum phenomenon. Quantum physics explains that discrete units of energy (the word *quanta* means "packets of energy") pop up in one place and then in another without going through the space in between. To grasp this rather illogical reality, picture a "quantum ball" about to fall from the top step of a stairway. The unique action of the quantum ball, says Amit Goswami in *The Self-Aware Universe*, has it on one step, then appearing on the next step *without* traversing the space in between. Such "quantum jumps" sound fantastic, but such activity precisely describes reality in the quantum realm.

Leadership is discontinuous. The field exists only as long as leaders have followers. Breaks exist between leadership events just as a motion picture is made up of separate frames and spaces exist between the letters in words such as:

l | e | a | d | e | r | s | h | i | p.

A leader who frequently and consistently attracts followers gives the appearance of leadership continuity. However, as Iacocca's and Jobs's up-and-down experience shows, leadership fields are tenuous. Followers join with a leader and break off; perhaps they will rejoin, or they may never commit to the leader again.

Because leadership is discontinuous, anyone can manifest a leadership event in the everyday activity of organizational life. Quantum discontinuity clarifies that leadership is not restricted to a select few high-visibility types. The leadership mantle can jump from one person to another as various leader-follower connections occur in the day-to-day, hour-to-hour, and minute-to-minute activities that form the foundation of most people's experience throughout organizations.

Focusing on the few high-profile individuals who continuously gain followers limits the concept of leadership. The assumption that high-visibility leaders represent the primary domain of leadership action intimidates people. Few can imitate the grand feats accomplished by those who function at the highest levels of government or business. Their experience is out of reach for most people. After all, how many people become president of a major corporation, serve at the head of a national government, lead a national social or religious movement, direct armies in significant battles, or ascend to other highly visible positions?

The concept of discontinuous leadership action helps today's flattened organizations, which focus on empowerment. Multiple leadership events need to occur in the deep fabric of corporate life: in one-on-one interactions on the shop floor, in conversations held in open office spaces, in small-group meetings, in all departments of every organization, as well as in the top-floor suites of corporate boards and in the high-level meetings of heads of state. Whether people toil on the loading dock or spend their time in the boardroom, knowing they can create a leadership event if only for a day, an hour, or a moment empowers them, and it adds to the organization's sum total of leadership.

> *Action Idea: Multiply the leadership events.* Multiply the quanta of leadership power that pop up throughout your organization by recognizing every leadership event regardless of its scope or duration. Make it clear to others that many diverse occurrences of leader-follower fields demonstrate leadership. Show people that being a leader is not a continuous reality owned by a select few, and encourage them to gain followers-allies in small-group meetings and in other day-to-day events.

> *Action Idea: Pass the ball.* Leadership power expands when it is shared. Pass your support to others by becoming a willing follower when their initiatives prove worthy. Relinquish your lead when someone else steps up with an

idea that has merit. Reward others for their stints as leaders even if the event is very brief. Honor the discontinuous nature of leadership as not only acceptable but highly valued, especially if your organization has flattened its hierarchy. This effort will encourage more people to take the kind of initiative that becomes essential when companies restructure.

Action Idea: Get past high-visibility media leadership mania. The preoccupation with high-visibility media leaders limits an organization's ability to take advantage of the full potential of its people. Recognize that those who make the front pages and are featured on the nightly news represent only a small portion of total leadership potential. Educate those in your organization that the select few who frequently and consistently take action are aligning with the same natural laws of leadership that govern any initiative, which means everyone can take a leadership role.

Leadership Influence as a Force vs. an Interaction

Leadership creates the energy that moves an organization. The philosopher Bertrand Russell noted that "the fundamental concept in social science is power, in the same sense in which energy is the fundamental concept in physics." Power is the currency leaders use to influence others.

Leadership Influence as a Force

Leaders are typically portrayed as captains of industry and heads of state who can wield the power of the purse or enforce their will through military might. In organizations, people commonly view their bosses or managers as leaders because of the formal authority of the position. Yet being a boss or a manager does not make someone a leader. We have all known bosses who could not lead us to the water fountain even if we needed a drink.

Influence as force derives from the classical physics world of visible, measurable matter. Classical physics describes nature's forces as propelling things through space by overcoming other inhibiting forces, such as inertia and friction. This kind of influence is an energy-exhausting process: Matter wears out; it gets tired and loses its clarity. In the same way, managers who rely on the force of formal authority experience a physical and emotional drain. They constantly work against the drag of opposing forces in the form of political battles over "turf," complaints from subordinates that "it's not my job," and blocking tactics such as "we've never done it that way before."

Leadership Influence as an Interaction

Leadership fields occur through commitment, not force. Commitment occurs because of the quality of the interaction between leaders and followers.

At the quantum level, the mere association of information-energy transforms the energy and creates unlimited possibilities. Influence in the quantum realm results from interaction. The self-interacting dynamics of the field translate potentialities into actualities. As a medium of interaction, the power of the field resides in its relational qualities, its interconnectedness.

Quantum Leadership indicates that a leader's influence does not depend upon force but dwells in what Margaret Wheatley, in her book *Leadership and the New Science*, calls a "medium of connection." Leaders gain followers-allies through influence based on interactions beyond formal authority *(the fourth natural law of leadership)*. They foster trust and mutual respect, so they attract followers. No one can force others to follow willingly. Leadership fields represent an interaction of human information-energy—an invisible reality or spatial geometry of motivation to work together. Leadership influence resembles laser light—a transformation of separate light beams into a coherent interaction pattern of multiple light waves. And coherent laser light can cut through the hardest materials. The extraordinary impact of leadership occurs because leadership influence represents a powerful bond of human interaction.

The fact that we do not always look at leadership influence as interaction provides one explanation why we lack leaders. Many presume they need formal authority to lead. I often hear comments such as, "I don't have the authority to do that," or, "I have to get approval before I can do anything." Quantum Leadership directs people to go beyond formal authority. It guides them to create the real power of leadership by developing the necessary quality of interaction that attracts others to follow.

Influence as interaction also shows us how to lead in the era of the revolutionary change we face today. The simultaneous revolutions of economic globalization, organizational reengineering, information technology, and workforce diversification have strained the utility of formal authority as the way to get things done. Frequent, rapid change destroys the legitimacy of prescribed stations of power. As people cut across national borders, create new processes to accomplish work, access information instantly, and work with people unlike themselves, reliance on position-to-position influence impedes progress. Person-to-person influence becomes paramount as traditional hierarchies of authority break down.

As organizations move toward self-directed work teams, the key question of who leads when no one is in charge can be answered by recognizing that "being in charge" does not confer leadership. Those who succeed in transformational times will develop influence beyond authority as the basis of their impact on organizations.

Leadership influence as interaction also defines how leaders master the locus of their power. Quantum Leaders interact with their environment to determine a course of action; they interact with followers to attract their support; and they interact with their consciousness, their "inner selves," to define their intentions, focuses of attention, choices, and directions of initiative.

Action Idea: Distinguish between managerial and leadership roles. Explain to others that the role of leader is distinct from the role of manager. The manager's role is to guide people to do what the organization defines as a job requirement, while the leader's role is to enter into the nonprescribed arena beyond rules and regulations. To reinforce the achievement of required responsibilities, label and reward the distinctive activities of managers who function as managers; to clarify the need for such action, reward managers who take initiative in the leader's arena. To increase the leadership in your organization, support and encourage nonmanagers who take the lead, and acknowledge their efforts.

Action Idea: Double your face-to-face contact frequency. The interaction that joins followers and leaders in a leadership event depends on the quality of interaction that already exists between them. Doubling face-to-face contact provides a structured way to develop positive interactions with others. Set aside time each week for such contact with each person in your area to improve the quality of interaction.

Action Idea: Analyze your interactions with the environment and with yourself. Quantum Leadership defines interaction as the key to leadership influence. Consider how you typically interpret and respond to information about problems and opportunities. Are you proactive or reactive? Do you engage in situations, or do you tend to analyze from a distance? After considering your typical pattern of interaction, ask yourself, "How does my approach serve me?" If you realize you can do better by changing your interaction with the environment, try a different approach.

Conduct the same analysis for your interactions with yourself, your inner world of thoughts and feelings, the internal sense of "I" from which you view the world. How clear are you regarding your intentions? What can you do to be clearer? What do you typically pay attention to and why? How can you improve your focus of attention? How do you decide what events mean? What could you do to refine your discrimination? How could you create more choices?

Finding the answers to these questions will take some reflection. Spend a few minutes each day analyzing your interactions, and keep notes to track your ideas. Over time you will improve the quality of your interaction with the environment and with yourself, which will propel you to greater leadership power.

Leadership Cause and Effect vs. Unpredictability

In 1994, the American Management Association found that 66 percent of companies that downsized reported *no* increases in productivity, and 55 percent of downsized companies had *no* gains in operating profits. Furthermore, 80 percent of the down-sized companies surveyed admitted that the employees who remained were suffering from low morale.

I imagine that in each case, someone in these rightsized organizations used cause-and-effect logic to demonstrate how personnel cutbacks would boost profits and productivity.

Predictability and certainty create a sense of stability and security. Most efforts to rationalize work, to define procedures, and to "get organized" are based on the belief that these actions will bring about specific results.

Cause-and-Effect Leadership Logic

Newton perceived reality as a great ticking clock set in unceasing, predictable motion and propelled by deterministic forces. Central to his worldview is the assumption that events occur because of cause and effect—that predictable, deterministic forces govern the action of matter. If you roll a billiard ball to your left, it moves in a predictable line. If it collides with other billiard balls, specific and measurable forces determine their paths and the speed of all resulting motion. However, cause-

and-effect thinking restricts people's ability to change because it creates the belief that an approach or strategy that worked well in the past will work again. To operate in the leadership arena, we must transcend the limits of the clockworks reality.

Leadership Unpredictability

Leaders operate in a messy world. The Quantum Leadership paradigm accounts for the unpredictable, uncertain, nondeterministic reality of leadership. In the quantum world, packets of energy or quanta fluctuate in odd ways. They leap from one place to another with no certainty about where or when they will make the jump, and they do not obey the linear logic of Newton's reality. Quantum fields are not subject to deterministic laws of force or pressure. You cannot predict a field's specific behavior, regardless of how much you know about it. Yet the quantum domain is not random chaos. Interactions occur in globally recognizable patterns, although localized action does not repeat along exactly the same paths. As in a gambling casino, probabilities govern the patterns of quantum action.

Quantum Leadership shows us that leaders operate in an uncharted arena outside the predictable lines defined by deterministic rules and standard operating procedures *(the fifth natural law of leadership)*. Leaders offer direction when people do not know how to solve problems, and they plot action steps when people fail to recognize or do not know how to exploit opportunities. The leadership arena is, by definition, an unknowable theater of action.

The unpredictability of the quantum casino means that risk is ever-present. Likewise, leadership always involves taking a "risk of initiative" *(the sixth natural law of leadership)*. The "correctness" of any voyage into the risk and uncertainty of the leadership arena is always unclear. The probability that the leader will identify a successful path depends on his or her interaction with the environment. The probability that he or she can influence and gain the commitment of followers depends on their interaction. Some may follow, and others may not *(the seventh natural law of leadership)*.

The unpredictability and risk that attach to leadership explains why some organizations experience a leadership vacuum. A desire for certainty focuses on establishing fail-safe mechanisms. Since the leadership arena cannot be controlled using this approach, people shy away. Simply put, people are unwilling to take necessary risks.

But in an era of change, uncertainty abounds. No one can escape the perilous impact of revolutionary change. Leaders accept risk and uncertainty as part of the territory. They adopt a mind-set of paying careful attention to their surroundings and of finely tuned discrimination about choices. And then leaders act. Their intention to lead drives them to take risks. Quantum Leadership transcends the fail-safe approach in favor of the belief that it is safe to fail. It accepts the unpredictability of leadership, and shuns cookbook suggestions about how to lead. Quantum Leadership provides choices for action, not prescriptions.

> *Action Idea: Let go of cause-and-effect thinking once in awhile.* To let go of cause-and-effect thinking means to suspend the belief in a cause-and-effect sequence of actions. Use information as a springboard to explore nonlinear leaps of logic. For example, instead of assuming that Plan A will result in Outcome B, play with the idea that Plan A will create outcome Not-B, Outcome X, and/or Outcome Z. By using this thinking, you may become aware of new possibilities that are more appropriate to discern behavior in the Quantum Leadership arena. Letting go of cause-and-effect thinking helps us continually learn and adapt to information rather than force information into predetermined logic.

> *Action Idea: Look for global patterns.* Accepting the idea of unpredictability does not mean adopting the view that there is nothing but hopeless chaos. Global patterns do exist in the quantum realm, and leaders can use them as a

guide to action. Look for global patterns, but do not be fooled into thinking they will duplicate in exactly the same, deterministic manner every time. Rather, look for the global nonlinear patterns—those that repeat, but rarely (in any specific case) along exactly the same lines.

For example, in the process redesign work I do for organizations, I observe the following global pattern of behavior. People first recognize the value in outlining the process used to accomplish a task; then they experience a backlash against the procedure. They complain that there are too many steps, and so they resist the work because it is impossible to figure out what all the steps are. The causes behind this global pattern vary: perhaps a lack of understanding of how work gets done, an unwillingness to think the process through, or a desire to keep work habits secret to maintain personal control.

And the results of this global pattern vary as well: People act out various conflicts, they fail to complete the assignment, they go off on a tangent about "other problems" that they believe are more serious. I am never certain what will happen in any specific process redesign effort because even small changes in certain conditions can create major changes. However, the underlying global pattern remains clear. People recognize the value, they experience backlash, they complain, they resist, but it plays out differently each time. Armed with awareness of this aperiodic pattern, I am able to respond to my clients in more effective ways. I understand order exists in chaos, but I am not fooled into thinking the order unfolds in a routine way.

Leadership as Objective vs. Subjective

Leadership unpredictability does not mean that you throw the dice or spin the roulette wheel and simply hope. In the quantum casino, leaders have an ace up their sleeve. The ace has a subjective face based in consciousness or how information is processed.

Leadership as Objective

Most approaches to leadership emerge from the assumption of an objective reality where the observer stands separate from the observed. Newton's physics suggests that the predictable world of matter exists "out there," independent of interference by your scrutiny and that we are passive witnesses to an objective and material reality acted upon by propelling and restraining forces.

The belief that leadership is an objective reality results in efforts to define traits, behaviors, habits, and attributes as supposed indicators of a leader. Prescriptions for "effective" leadership attempt to define impartial standards that are supposed to exist. However, the objective approach does not apply to leadership. Consider how two politicians can explain the same situation in totally different ways, and how two voters can respond to the same politician in completely opposite ways. Note how two business managers might use the same data to evaluate a problem and come up with diametrically opposed solutions.

Leadership as Subjective

Leadership is a subjective reality based in the consciousness of the leader and his or her followers. For example, an air force base was experiencing the shock waves of change caused by their uncertain role since the end of the cold war, the impending reductions in forces, and the tightening squeeze of funding cutbacks. In one meeting, the participants got into a heated argument about whether the base general was a leader. One colonel argued in favor of the general, citing three of his "leadership" characteristics: a sense of the big picture, good communication skills, and a high level of self-esteem. The civilians strongly disagreed. They felt the general lacked empathy and did not display a deep concern for those who were facing difficult changes. It was clear that both the colonel and the civilians were stuck in the assumption that leadership was an objective reality based on visible parts. They failed to recognize that their subjective consciousness, their self-referral information processing, defined leadership. Had they understood this, they could have explained the interaction between the general and others and would have realized why he gained some people as followers but not others.

The Quantum Leadership paradigm explains that reality is subjective. Consciousness—how people process information—creates meaning. Consciousness translates potentiality—what could be—into probabilities for action—what we decide is. Quantum physics shows that the interaction of your consciousness with your surroundings makes you an active participant-creator of your reality. You affect what you observe. What you observe depends on what you choose to observe. And your interpretation depends on your subjective information processing. Your act of observation and interpretation alters the world.

This notion goes against most of our education. We learned the "correct labels" for things, people, and events, and we were programmed to believe in certain "objective truths" that were "proved" by the scientific method. Our belief in objectivity exists by virtue of the "correctness," "truth," and "proofs" we were taught.

Yet "proven" truths can be invalid hoaxes. For thirty years science fully accepted that the bone fragments of a supposed prehistoric human, labeled Piltdown Man, represented the missing link between apes and humans. Later investigation found that the remains were merely carefully doctored evidence planted to promote a hoax. Supposedly proven truths can also be dangerously wrong. Thalidomide was supposed to be a boon for pregnant women, but the drug turned out to cause severe birth defects in the fetus. DDT was supposed to save food crops from insects at no danger to humans, but subsequent study uncovered the damaging impact the pesticide had on human health. The expansion of human awareness changed these "realities."

Consciousness creates leadership *(the eighth natural law of leadership)* because leaders and followers unite according to how they process information in any situation. When consciousness connects, a shared reality exists. Followers accept the leader, and the leadership field manifests itself. The field is a self-referential identity with the leader's and followers' consciousness *(the ninth natural law of leadership)*.

Wal-Mart employees loved Sam Walton, and the Green Bay Packer players were devoted to coach Vince Lombardi because the employees and players, respectively, identified with their leaders. Self-referral explains that the leader and follower are reflections of each other.

Quantum physics indicates that consciousness serves as the creative element and causal agent of the universe, and that makes consciousness infinitely more important than matter. Our consciousness subjectively filters how we receive information, how we interpret that information, and how we respond to it. In terms of leadership, the quantum mechanics of this self-referral leadership process begin when a spark of the leader's consciousness perceives the need for action in a particular direction.

For example, in 1991, Louis Katopodis, president of Fiesta Mart, a Houston-based grocery chain, saw the opportunity to expand the organization into other cities in Texas. His subjective interpretation of the environment energized him to propose a direction. When this happens, the leader in effect says, "Follow me this way." For Katopodis that meant convincing the board of directors and the senior management group to open new stores in three cities—Austin, Beaumont, and Dallas. The meaning of the leader's direction exists within the leader.

A similar spark of consciousness must occur within the followers-allies. They subjectively evaluate the leader and the leader's direction and respond, "Yes, I will follow," signaling an acceptance of and connection with the leader. The sparks of leader- and follower-consciousness ignite to form the leadership field. Leader and followers perceive the situation from a similar perspective. They unify their consciousness and become one mind—an alliance of awareness, mutually committed to a direction. In this connection the power of leadership bursts forth.

The connection of leader-follower consciousness is analogous to tuning the dial on a radio. When listeners turn the dial to the proper frequency, they make a connection and the sound comes in clearly. When they miss the channel, only static comes through. Leadership influence occurs when the leader and follower tune in on a similar wavelength of awareness. The connection is nonmaterial. Quantum Leadership influence is consciousness connecting in an invisible spatial geometry that binds people together. In *Microcosm*, George Gilder explains this quantum reality of life: "Physicists now agree that matter derives from waves, fields, and probabilities. To comprehend nature, we have to stop thinking of the world as basically material and begin imagining it as a manifestation of consciousness."

I observe the quantum connection of subjective consciousness at all organizational levels and throughout all organizational areas. People make a commitment to follow or align with someone in circumstances that range from large-scale, company-wide strategic efforts to very specific projects that affect small groups or a few people at a particular workstation.

The quantum connection was evident at Fiesta when Katopodis gained the necessary commitment of followers to his direction. One top manager told me, "Louis really knows what he's doing." When I asked what that meant, he replied, "Well, Louis made a lot of sense because I thought there were good opportunities in each of the three cities Louis wanted to move into. I thought Louis was on the right track, and I felt comfortable with his plan of action." The manager's statements reveal that the self-referral, subjective consciousness of the follower creates the leadership connection.

A universe without objectivity does not mean that standards do not exist. Through the lens of the Quantum Leadership paradigm, we see that leaders reflect the standards of both their self-referral consciousness and the collective, self-referential consciousness of the followers-allies. People do not follow or align with those whom they perceive as alien to themselves. When a person gives expression to a direction, it reveals the quality of the person's intentions and discrimination. If the direction resonates in some consistent way with another's self-referral awareness, they will follow. The meaning of the direction exists within the leader, and the meaning of the leader exists within the follower. By referring back to themselves, leaders determine direction in their own image, and followers create the leader in their own image. Thus, leadership standards exist within the leader's and followers' consciousness.

This does not mean that all leaders are benevolent. Leaders who operate from a less evolved state of consciousness can chart a course that is divisive or destructive, and they can attract followers who have self-referral with such action. The nine natural laws of leadership are descriptive; they define what leaders are rather than what they should be. Yet we want leaders who have high standards and are compassionate, competent, and life supporting. The Quantum Leadership paradigm provides a means of prescribing how to lead in a more enlightened manner. The key is the expansion of consciousness.

Specific expressions of consciousness such as thoughts are manifestations of an underlying source of awareness. Thoughts define what we are conscious of. For example, you are conscious of the words on this page. Those thoughts indicate that you have the capacity to be conscious. That is, a source of awareness or ground state of pure consciousness exists within. The source of consciousness is like a well from which water can be drawn, and a specific expression of consciousness is like a bucket of water drawn from the well. If the flow of well water is cut off or blocked in some way, we cannot receive the water. If the flow of awareness from pure consciousness is blocked, the leader's energy, creativity, and intelligence cannot be fully expressed. Furthermore, if expressions of consciousness are programmed along narrow, divisive, or negative lines, the leader's thinking and action can be restricted, divisive, or destructive. The hope for more enlightened leaders lies in expanding the access and increasing the flow from the source of consciousness within us.

The expansion of consciousness means enhancing the flow of pure consciousness, which is accomplished in two ways. First, the capacity to process information must be increased by improving the conductor or circuitry of consciousness—the level of mind-body fitness or our neurophysiological efficiency. When a leader's mind and body are dull, tired, or undernourished, consciousness does not move very well, and he or she lacks the energy, creativity, and intelligence to operate in the challenging leadership arena. Second, the flow of pure consciousness is enhanced by transcending the limits of programmed and conditioned thinking and action. When limited frames of reference and prejudicial bias filter awareness, when alternate interpretations of reality are discarded or unnoticed, awareness of opportunities is restricted and recognition of alternatives to overcoming obstacles is limited. Leaders then fail to map the territory to identify possibilities and problems, and they do not chart courses of action that lead to success.

As consciousness expands, our relationship to the world changes because our self-referral identity expands. Expanded consciousness enhances the sense of unity; we recognize the interdependencies that underlie apparent diversity. Expanded consciousness increases our sense of responsibility; we are more able to respond. Expanded consciousness changes the reference point; we no longer see ourselves in the world but see the world in ourselves.

Action Idea: Cultivate greater mind-body coherence. Our state of consciousness depends on our mental and physical states. We think more clearly when the brain works in a more orderly way, and physically, we feel more energetic when the physical body operates in a more fluid fashion. Our self-referral consciousness reflects our mind-body coherence. We are more open to possibilities, more able to adapt to change, and more capable of overcoming obstacles when mind-body coherence is greater. Diet, exercise, rest, sleep, and lifestyle all affect this coherence. Consider what and how you eat, the extent and frequency of exercise you do, the quality and quantity of rest and sleep you get, and the lifestyle habits you have. Do they enable you to be more or less conscious? Do they promote more or less capacity to process information? By improving mind-body coherence, you increase your capacity to contact and draw from pure consciousness, your underlying power source, to be more conscious; this strengthens your ability to take the leadership.

Action Idea: Understand that a quantum leader is both a scientist and an artist. The science component is a set of definable laws that describe and explain the process: Gain followers; build relationships; recognize leadership events; seek to influence beyond authority; attend to the nonprescribed leadership arena; accept risk; and know that not everyone will follow. These are the mechanics or science of leadership. But applying the science requires a consideration of the complex, chaotic situations where finesse, creativity, judgment, and wisdom are required to do the right thing and to do things right. Information processing, consciousness, and self-referral are the brush and palette that leaders use to artistically construct their leadership reality. Effective Quantum Leadership means keeping the mechanics in mind and applying consciousness in ever more expansive and adaptive ways. Pasteur noted that "chance favors those who are prepared for it." Quantum Leadership offers an understanding and methodology to prepare for the future and put chance on our side.

4

Enlightened Leaders for a Quantum Age

"The quantum era is still unfolding . . . in a transformation of the world."

—*George Gilder, author of* Microcosm

Quantum Leadership represents a more complete approach to leading than the perspective based on Newtonian assumptions. It meets the realities of a competitive business environment and adds value to leadership practice because it offers a model that guides leaders to function in a more enlightened and life-supporting manner.

Competitive Business Realities

We live in a quantum era. Today, organizations must compete using an integrated, field view of the environment. "Go global or die" is heard throughout all major industries as companies face an interconnected worldscape—a global field—of business markets. Companies operating in this marketplace need a switchboardlike network of linkages—fields of interaction that consolidate local areas and then unify the organization into a whole with larger fields. The economic globalization and unification of previously fragmented markets requires today's leaders to operate with a "whole world mind."

Organizations recognize they can no longer operate as independent parts. Team-based organizational structures are essential as organizations rightsize, restructure, and reinvent themselves. Quality, service, and organizational process problems and opportunities are now viewed as systemic, not as localized issues. Flattened hierarchies and worker empowerment demand multiple leaders rather than reliance on formal authority and prescribed, deterministic modes of operating. Cross-functional work teams represent consciousness unified into fields of coherent action. In *Managing on the Edge*, Richard T. Pascali recounts that during the 1980s, Ford's president, Don Peterson, recognized that if he were to lead Ford to build world-class cars, he needed to unite all aspects of the company into a unified field. Peterson understood that Ford's

> "manufacturing problem" wasn't a *manufacturing* problem alone. For manufacturing to work effectively, it had to be tied closely to the other organizational functions. What was necessary was a thorough-going transformation of virtually all aspects of the company—including a greater involvement of sales, marketing, design, engineering, and finance; a rebalancing of power between the line and staff functions; increased levels of participation by individual workers and their unions; and the redesign of central control systems, communication networks, corporate values, and strategy. Ford regarded these shifts as requiring *discontinuous* change.

Peterson saw the fundamental power of a unified approach over a separate parts approach. His efforts paid off. Ford's share of the U.S. auto market increased from 16 percent in 1980 to 22 percent in 1987, and new quality standards in Ford's manufacturing processes steered it from poorest to number one among the Big Three automakers.

Peterson's reference to discontinuous change strikes a familiar chord that reverberates throughout today's competitive arena. The rapid pace of environmental and technological change means that incremental, one-foot-following-the-other goals and action plans do not work during periods of abrupt transformation. A key standard for success in the 1990s is "stretch targets"—gigantic, seemingly unreachable milestones—which drive leader to take dramatic leaps forward and reinvent how they do business.

Command-and-control tactics are now being replaced by reliance on commitment as the basis for effective influence. Self-directed work teams rely on the interaction of their members to guide the group's activity. The increase of workforce diversity means that organizations can no longer simply demand that people assimilate and fit themselves into a "traditional" ethnic/gender mold. Successful organizations must carefully cultivate commitment by using coaching and development to guide employee behavior. Partnering with suppliers, customers, and producers has become commonplace as organizations rely on positive interaction as a means to competitive success.

Traditional notions of predictability and stability have been shattered. By 1991, only fourteen of the original fifty-two companies rated as "excellent" in a 1982 study by Tom Peters and Bob Waterman could still be categorized in this way. Furthermore, 42 percent of the 1992 Fortune 500 companies were not classified in that elite group in 1991. No company has an ensured lock on market success, and no company holds an industry position so dominant that it can buffer dynamic change. In the late 1980s, that impregnable fortress IBM swooned under the heat of intense competition from smaller companies. By 1992, "Big Blue" proved to be too sluggish and inflexible for the rapidly changing information processing marketplace.

People are not separate observers of an objective world. The quantum, nonmaterial, and invisible reality of human information processing capacity determines competitive success. Subjective perception *is* reality. Quality products and services are defined by the customer's point of view. Intellectual capital, which is structured in the individual and collective consciousness of the workforce, is today's new competitive advantage.

The invisible power of the mind takes precedence over matter. The truth wealth of nations is in creative brain power, not in material resources such as buildings and balance sheets. Information-energy supplants solid matter as a greater power. "Traditional fuels are congealed resources—the coal, coke, and iron that go into make an ingot of steel—put together with a bit of know-how. New products—like software and advanced aircraft—are," according to a January 14, 1991, article in *Fortune* magazine, "congealed knowledge bound up in a bit of material." Successful organizations in this interconnected, discontinuously changing, unpredictable world driven by subjective perception require Quantum Leaders—men and women who embrace the uncertainty of the leadership arena and rely on the development of consciousness as the real power of leadership.

The Quantum Leadership Model

Quantum Leadership offers a practical model for guiding all leaders so that they can provide enlightened, life-supporting solutions to overcome problems and exploit opportunities. Quantum Leadership practice compares to a game set on a broadly defined playing field in which the play changes as it unfolds and its players interact. The Quantum Leadership model guides leadership practice by defining the underlying, stable interactions and by offering choices to create these interactions.

Figure 4-1 depicts the Quantum Leadership model. The model defines three essential interactions that make up the process.

1. *The Quantum Leader–leadership arena interaction.* The arrow that arcs from the Quantum Leader up to the leadership arena designates this interaction. Quantum Leaders create this

Figure 4-1. The Quantum Leadership model.

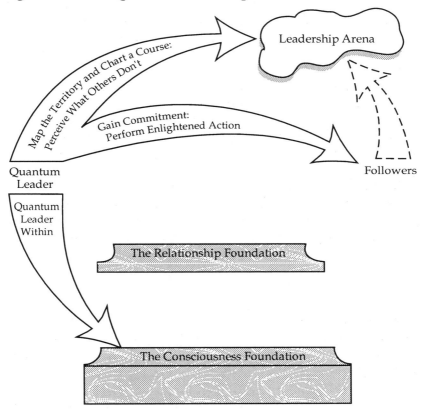

interaction when they map the territory—perceive possibilities or identify problems in the leadership arena—and chart a course—establish a path that exploits opportunities or resolves problems—by perceiving what others do not.

2. *The Quantum Leader–follower interaction.* The arrow that connects the Quantum Leader and followers specifies this interaction. Quantum Leaders create this connection when they gain commitment by performing enlightened action. The quality of relationship forms the foundation that underlies the Quantum Leader–follower interaction.

3. *The Quantum Leader–consciousness interaction.* The arrow between the Quantum Leader and the consciousness foundation indicates this interaction. Quantum Leaders self-refer to their consciousness, their information processing source, and they express consciousness as the components that define the Quantum Leader within, the particular structure of their consciousness.

The dotted arrow that connects the follower with the leadership arena illustrates the end result of the three interactions. Followers join the leader and venture into the leadership arena.

Mapping the Territory and Charting a Course: Perceiving What Others Don't

The arrow in Figure 4-1 arcing up from the Quantum Leader to the leadership arena shows how Quantum Leaders direct their consciousness to interact with the vague, uncertain territory outside prescribed boundaries. Quantum Leaders map the territory and then chart a course. These processes define how Quantum Leaders operate outside the prescribed boundaries *(the fifth natural law of leadership).*

Consider how Martha Hahn, then Associate State Director for Colorado, mapped the territory and charted a course during a 1993 meeting of the Bureau of Land Management (BLM) Field Committee, a group made up of BLM managers from all parts of the United States. The meeting's purpose was to identify issues critical to the bureau's mission. Hahn's concern was the growing diversity of the public the bureau served—increasing numbers of women, Hispanics, and other minorities using BLM services offered at federal parks and in federal recreation areas. Yet the BLM was traditionally weak in its ability to recruit, maintain, and then promote women into its upper ranks. Hahn believed the BLM had to revamp its practices, so she charted a course to resolve the problem: Audit the bureau's culture, and identify exactly what the BLM needed to do differently regarding its practices with women employees.

Quantum Leaders perceive what others don't when they

map the territory and chart a course. That means that their awareness has the distinctive quality of a more insightful level of consciousness. People typically do not need direction when they know what to do or when they know how to do it. Whether they are right or wrong, if they firmly believe they are on the correct course, they usually do not seek guidance, nor will they heed it. Quantum Leaders become important when uncertainty clouds people's awareness and people do not know what to do. Anyone can recognize a blazing forest fire. The real skill lies in sniffing out the first smoke. Quantum Leaders also become valuable when they can demonstrate a superior course of action that others do not recognize.

During the BLM meeting, Hahn raised the women's issue while the group brainstormed about potentially important topics. During the discussion of issues, Hahn explained her idea: "We need to look at our procedures for responding to women within BLM, and then we need to improve them." "That's pretty straightforward," one committee member retorted. "We know how to do that." Many of the field committee members obviously agreed with this comment, because someone else raised a point on a different topic, and the group began discussing it. Hahn challenged the group. "I think that's part of the problem," she stated easily but firmly. "We have approached this as a simple issue, but it isn't. Complex cultural forces and deeply rooted biases have limited our ability to deal with the issue effectively."

Hahn's comments reveal how perceiving what others don't might be a new, innovative insight for others. Her perception was unique; it clarified that existing BLM approaches had not met the organization's need and had also masked the need for a new direction.

Perceiving what others don't might be an idea that was lost, forgotten, or not timely in a previous circumstance. Ronald Reagan's successful run for the presidency in 1980 was based on ideas that were almost identical to the approach to government he had first extolled in 1964 and had maintained throughout his political career. In 1980, Reagan mapped the territory and charted a course to reintroduce possibilities that had been dormant, forgotten, or unacceptable to the majority of Americans. In business, perceiving what others don't may also mean simply reintroducing lost or forgotten ideas in response to business cycles. Consider an organization in which someone takes the initiative and gets support to expand operations, such as adding a new production line. Then, over time, someone gains backing for trimming expenses, such as reducing labor. Developing new production lines and instituting labor cutbacks are not new or radical innovations. Yet they become fodder for leadership because the person who perceives them does so at a time when the directives are relevant to the organization and no one else has recognized the need for such action.

Quantum Leaders perceive what others don't in order to step ahead of the pack and guide them forward. Quantum Leadership describes the choices available for doing this (see Chapter 6). These processes involve the leader's capacity to gain another perspective of awareness, which I refer to as "going into the G.A.P."—the place where the leader *g*ains *a*nother *p*erspective.

Quantum Leaders must think differently from others. They must direct their awareness along channels of information processing that go beyond heavy reliance on Newtonian logic. Quantum Leadership explains how leaders go into the G.A.P., which enables the Quantum Leader to break the boundaries that limit and misdirect perception of the leadership arena. By gaining another perspective, Quantum Leaders open themselves to new ways of observing, interpreting, and evaluating information. This allows their awareness to recognize patterns of intelligence, order, and possibility that provide new approaches to action. Gaining another perspective equips Quantum Leaders to interact with the leadership arena beyond the confines created by restricted attention and by conditioned, limited perception. Operating from the G.A.P. illustrates how the leader's consciousness creates leadership *(the eighth natural law of leadership)*. Martha Hahn was in the G.A.P. when she identified the impact of BLM's cultural roots and recognized the need to audit current practices. Quantum Leadership describes specific techniques to guide awareness into the G.A.P. (see Chapter 7).

The Quantum Leader–Follower Interaction

Gaining Commitment: Performing Enlightened Action

Once Quantum Leaders identify a course of action, they need to gain willing followers *(the first natural law of leadership)*. To gain follower commitment, they perform enlightened action: They enlighten followers to recognize and accept the leader's course of action. Performing enlightened action is analogous to turning on a light to show the way in a pitch-black room. The leader's message enlightens followers to support and venture forth with the leader.

Recall that Martha Hahn's comments about issues regarding women in the BLM were initially passed over by the group. Hahn had to challenge the field committee to recognize that the women's issue was in fact a problem. Her comments rang true with Bill Calkins, then Associate State Director of Alaska, who chimed in, "Martha's right." It took additional action to win over the rest of the group. After Calkins indicated his agreement with Hahn, a lengthy discussion ensued about different interpretations of the problem, and Hahn had to break into the group's discussion again.

"I need to make a point," she commented thoughtfully. "We're just rehashing what we already know. We need to act now and launch a new direction, not simply talk and retalk issues. We don't need more talk; we need action."

"Well, what should we do?" Calkins asked Hahn. Everyone looked directly at her. She spoke clearly:

"We need to assess the hiring and recruitment process that we now use. I suggest we form a quality team to outline our process. Then we can find ways to improve it. We also need to clearly identify the specific needs of women already in BLM to help us determine the actions that will better serve them. I suggest we develop and administer a survey of the staff as soon as possible."

These statements catalyzed the group. "Let's do it," Calkins replied, and the entire committee nodded their agreement.

Martha Hahn effectively communicated her ideas because she had adapted her message to meet the needs of the situation. Quantum Leadership provides choices that increase communication flexibility—the capacity to use multiple channels—and improve communication congruence—the capacity to present a message with consistency. Ultimately, Hahn gained the field committee's commitment because the meaning of her ideas transferred to the committee members. She created a connection of consciousness. Hahn met the field committee at their self-referral level of consciousness *(the ninth natural law of leadership)*, the source of meaning creation, and led them to her level.

Quantum Leadership describes how performing enlightened action involves communication that creates shared meaning and influences followers at the level of consciousness. Meaning is created through values and the frames of reference people use. Quantum Leaders create shared meaning when they perform action that resonates with the followers' values and when they frame or reframe information from a reference point that followers understand and accept as worth supporting.

Prior to the BLM meeting, Calkins had already shared Hahn's interpretation of the BLM practices in dealing with minorities. Her statements gave clear expression to thoughts he already had, so it was easy to establish a shared sense of meaning with him. Hahn won over the rest of the group because her ideas resonated with key values of the field committee members. The BLM tradition included meeting individual needs, and the field committee members valued an action orientation. Hahn framed her leadership direction as a set of specific steps, which helped others understand her ideas and believe they were appropriate. She also created shared meaning by suggesting the use of quality teams, an accepted and valued approach in the BLM for resolving problems. Quantum Leadership offers techniques for creating shared meaning (see Chapter 9).

Values are important reflections of information processing in terms of the emotional level of meaning—what we care about. Frames of reference are important reflections of information processing in terms of the content and context of information—

our perspective. Enlightened action also involves a subtler form of influence that is beyond authority *(the fourth natural law of leadership)*. Quantum Leader influence occurs on the level of consciousness where people actually code raw data into meaningful information and when leaders match the specific internal information processing codes followers use to represent reality in their mind. Quantum Leaders speak the followers' private mental language—the language that determines the structure of information processing.

Martha Hahn matched the private mental language of many of the field committee members when she provided specific details on how to approach the diversity problem, instead of giving only a general overview. Her ideas made sense because these field committee members code information by details. That is, they accept and understand information more readily when it is provided in terms of particulars. Reliance on either details or generalities is one of the internal codes that make up a person's private mental language. Hahn connected with the field committee on their wavelength of consciousness because she tapped into the actual structure they used to code information. The Quantum Leadership model explains how to access the private mental language people use and how to influence others on this level (see Chapter 10).

The Relationship Foundation

Because the personal relationship defines the existing quality of interpersonal interaction between the leader and would-be followers, followers will not join the leader without the requisite relationship. Leadership *is* the relationship *(the second natural law of leadership)*.

During the BLM meeting, Bill Calkins was initially the strongest supporter of Martha Hahn's ideas. This was no accident. Long before the meeting, he had come to believe that diversity was a key issue for BLM. He also held Martha Hahn in high professional regard. Hahn and Calkins had an established, positive relationship, which made it easier for him to commit to her lead.

When would-be followers have no prior relationship with a potential leader, gaining commitment depends solely on the action the leader performs on the spot. It is difficult to develop high levels of trust and a strong sense of shared common ground in such circumstances. This reality partly explains why networking plays such an important role in business and why name recognition is so important in politics. Leaders do lose followers when the leader no longer offers a direction that they interpret as meaningful. They can also lose followers when the quality of relationship cracks. When the leader loses the followers' trust, the leadership event ends. Quantum Leadership defines how to continually build and reinforce relationships with others by establishing a common ground, providing valued resources, and developing trust and credibility (see Chapter 11).

The Quantum Leader-Consciousness Interaction

The Consciousness Foundation

Quantum Leadership is structured in consciousness. The entire process emerges from the way leaders and followers process information. Consciousness forms a foundation that underlies the entire Quantum Leadership model. Quantum Leaders cannot directly control a follower's consciousness, although they can influence it by performing enlightened action. But they can control their own consciousness. They can refer back to their own source of awareness, pure consciousness, and direct their thinking and action along the lines they choose. As Jack Welch, CEO of General Electric, declares, "Quantum thinking has to become a way of life."

Quantum Leader Within

Through self-referral, Quantum Leaders contact the leader within the internal architecture of awareness that guides thinking and action. The Quantum Leader within has four components: intention, attention, discrimination, and initiative.

The Quantum Leader within Martha Hahn was intent on taking the lead at the BLM Field Committee meeting. She focused her attention on a key issue she believed was critical to the bureau's future. Her discriminatory capacities defined the problem and identified practical choices for resolving it. She took initiative when she felt it was necessary to gain followers.

Quantum Leaders know they have 100 percent control over the four components of awareness that define their leadership efforts. Quantum Leadership provides practical guidance about how to take control and restructure the internal architecture of the leader within to be more conscious and enhance leadership (see Chapter 5). It offers a new motto for leaders:

I am conscious; therefore I can lead.

Action Idea: Become "field conscious." Mapping the territory and charting a course and gaining the commitment of willing followers demand focusing awareness on the full spectrum of interactions that occur within the model. Quantum Leadership cannot be understood by looking at it piecemeal and by isolating its parts. You cannot simply add up the elements to understand it. That type of consciousness might work for a V-8 engine or a clock radio, but it does not apply to leadership. Becoming field conscious means you need to pay attention to the connections that link the personal, social, political, economic, legal, and technical factors that affect the leadership arena. You need to recognize the myriad factors that have an impact on your interactions with followers. At times the field might encompass only the members of a small-group meeting and their issues. At other times, the field might encompass a more global sphere. Continually challenge yourself to be aware of the field—the interactions—not just the parts.

Action Idea: Meet followers at their level. To gain commitment through enlightened action, interact with followers at their level of consciousness. Consider how followers interpret the leadership arena. Find out how others typically take in, translate, and respond to information, and then present your leadership initiative in a message that matches their mode of information processing. Martha Hahn knew that the field committee was an action-oriented group that understood information in terms of details. By specifying the precise actions they should take, she met the group at their level and reinforced their level of consciousness. Armed with a clear direction, they were more willing to tackle the diversity issue.

Action Idea: Make it personal. Relationships lie at the heart of the interpersonal connection within the leader-follower field. Spend time making personal contact with people. "Personal" does not mean you have to develop interactions that are nonwork-related. For many people, work consumes a good portion of who they are. Find ways to personalize your contact with others by asking them what matters to them about work. Because Bob Crawford, CEO of fast-growing Brook Furniture Rental, recognizes the importance of interpersonal connection, he finds time to accompany members of his 150-person sales force when they call on accounts. Customer reaction to his visits is powerful and positive. They tell him he is the first company president to give them a personal touch.

Action Idea: Become aware of pure consciousness. Can you think of a time when you seemed to witness your thoughts from a quiet place within? Have you ever had the experience of not actually thinking anything but being exquisitely alert? Perhaps you have had such experiences, even if they were only very momentary. For some, such incidents sound like New Age claptrap. However, as people recognize the need to find a source of internal stability amid the chaos and complexity of modern life, introspection and time for reflection are gaining acceptance among forward-thinking members of organizations. Many people believe being aware means constantly thinking about something. Yet behind our thoughts exists a state of mind that is pure awareness.

Thinking, being *conscious of* something, depends on the capacity to be conscious, or the existence of pure consciousness, awareness itself. By contacting and experiencing the state of pure consciousness, the quality of information processing expands. Pure awareness represents the internal source reservoir of information processing potential. It can be compared to an ocean of awareness; thoughts represent only localized waves or even more localized drops of water. By contacting the source, we can take action from an expanded platform of awareness. Or as Lao-Tzu, the sixth century B.C. Chinese philosopher stated, "The way to do is to be."

Stanford University professors Michael Ray and Rochelle Myers, in their book *Creativity in Business,* recommend a specific set of yoga exercises known as Surya Namaskar to contact the inner resource of pure awareness. These simple bending and stretching postures relax the body so that the mind can also settle down to its source.

Meditation techniques are another effective way to experience pure consciousness. Several hundred scientific research studies on transcendental meditation (TM), as taught by Maharishi Mahesh Yogi, have shown that regular practice of TM improves practical indicators of information processing capacity such as reaction time, perceptual motor performance, learning ability, memory, creativity, and cognitive flexibility. Scientific research on TM also shows it improves brain wave coherence and the stability of the nervous system. By using a technique such as TM to refer to that pure consciousness level, you can expand the platform of awareness of the Quantum Leader within.

5

The Quantum Leader Within

"What lies behind us and what lies before us are small matters compared to what lies within us."

—*Ralph Waldo Emerson*

Dick Frazar, a mid-level manager in a large southwestern utility company, runs five miles every day. The positive impact of his daily regimen is obvious. Approaching fifty, Dick's face shines with youthful vigor, and his firm, well-proportioned physique moves with the fluid grace of a trained athlete. Yet the purpose of Dick's run extends beyond his desire for physical fitness. He uses the time to focus in on his consciousness and define the architecture of the Quantum Leader within him.

During the spring of 1993, Dick had a lot to think about while he ran along his daily route. His company had just completed a major downsizing effort and internal reorganization. He had been assigned the additional responsibility of directing a division that served as a liaison between outside customers and several company departments. His new division had been hit particularly hard by the downsizing. It had lost more than 20 percent of its staff, including all but one of its administrative support people. The disgruntled reaction by division members alone would have been enough to occupy Dick's thinking. His challenge was compounded by complaints from other departments that the group was a surly, hard-to-work-with crew that was not meeting company needs.

Dick's work to improve his new division began in his consciousness—his capacity to process information. The Quantum Leadership model defines the Quantum Leader–consciousness interaction as the starting place for leadership. Quantum Leadership is based in consciousness. Mapping the territory and charting a course in the leadership arena and gaining the commitment of willing followers are the overt, resultant activities that reflect the invisible content and character of the inner world of mind. During his daily run in the spring of 1993, Dick systematically configured and reconfigured the form and function of his awareness regarding how to lead his new division. He consciously established the foundation for taking a leadership role in the situation he faced.

The Source of the Quantum Leader Within

The Quantum Leadership model indicates that Quantum Leaders interact with their consciousness to contact their source of leading (Figure 5-1). The leader's capacity for mapping the territory and charting a course in the uncertain leadership arena requires lively consciousness.

Consciousness creates leadership *(the eighth natural law of leadership)*. Quantum Leaders express their consciousness using a particular structure, which has four components:

1. Intention
2. Attention
3. Discrimination
4. Initiative

The interaction among these four components creates the unique, subjective reality of the Quantum Leader's information

Figure 5-1. The Quantum Leadership model: The consciousness foundation.

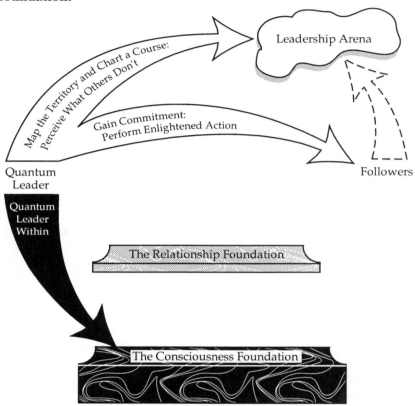

processing method (the leader's self-referral identity defined in *the ninth natural law of leadership*). The four components typically unfold sequentially: Intention guides attention; attention drives discrimination; discrimination directs initiative. Yet each component interacts with and reinforces the others as an interconnected network. The Quantum Leader within emerges from the sequential and simultaneous self-interacting dynamics of these four components.

Quantum Leader Intention

Leading begins with a *conscious intention*—the innermost core of the leader's purpose, desire, motivation, and values. Intention forms the foundation for the energy allocated to any endeavor. As Charles de Gaulle once said, "Nothing great will ever be achieved without great men, and men are great only if they are determined to be so." Quantum Leaders distinguish themselves because, first and foremost, they have the intention to lead. They enter situations—one-on-one interactions, small-group tasks, organization-wide efforts, and long-term ventures—with the desire to step into the risk zone of uncertainty and influence others to follow.

Intention has organizing power. It defines the platform of consciousness on which all other thinking and action rest. Quantum Leaders consciously clarify their intention in each circumstance they encounter to reaffirm their desire to lead and refine the purpose that guides them. When intention is foggy or uncertain, doubt inhibits the desire to lead. Don Williams, president of Trammell Crow, explained the need for the clarity of intention in today's changing global economy to *Fortune* magazine (April 19, 1993): "Life today is fired at us point blank. People don't have time to refer to the Bible or to the company handbook. You've got to have all of that internalized."

Establishing the Intention to Lead

Dick Frazar was clear about his intention: immediate action. He recognized that he had to deal with the unhappiness created by the downsizing. He knew he needed to address the dysfunctional conflict between members of the division caused by what some perceived as inequities in the distribution of work assignments. A history of poor communication practices among division members made it hard even to talk about these issues. In addition, he realized that the frequent complaints from other departments—complaints that revealed that his division was creating company-wide performance problems because it was not serving its internal customers—had to be resolved.

It may seem that Dick's intention was obvious and that anyone else in his place would have had a similar purpose. However, two other managers at his company provide an interesting contrast. Both had worked with the division for several years before Dick arrived. Both were well aware of the division's behavior and its poor relationship with other departments. Nevertheless, they felt no need to address the issue. One manager even criticized Dick for his efforts, saying they were not necessary.

Dick's example reveals how Quantum Leaders are consciously intent on making a difference rather than accepting something less. Robert Nelson, a store manager at Fiesta Mart, the Houston-based grocer, also displayed this quality of intention. In 1993, Fiesta established a new performance development system for its store and department managers. The first phase of the program required managers to work with their employees in a comprehensive program of goal setting, feedback, coaching, and appraisal sessions. A week after the system was rolled out, Nelson took action that extended beyond the prescribed implementation boundaries. In a 1993 interview, he explained his intention:

> This system offers a powerful tool. I can reward excellent individual performance and root out the cause of problems in my store. I know that the system will help me if I know how I am doing. I asked my department managers to give me feedback as part of the overall process. Their input will help me improve my approach to evaluating and developing others.

A program in which personnel receive feedback from their supervisor, peers, and subordinates was part of the second stage of the performance development process. Nelson's intention spurred him on to take that step right away, despite the fact that he had to put additional effort into an already time-consuming process.

Quantum Leader intention does not require years of soul searching, nor does it involve magical powers. You only have to look within yourself and ask, "What is my intention now?" Your immediate answer will tell all. If your clear intention is to lead, you will ignite the first sparks that will direct your consciousness into the leadership arena and gain willing followers.

The First Failure of Leadership

The first failure is the lack of conscious intention to lead. Without the propelling force of intention, movement stalls, motivation evaporates, and the leader cannot overcome obstacles or take advantage of opportunities.

A 1992 *USA Today* survey by Marcia Staimer asked executives from five industries, "Is your company committed to quality?" The percentage in each industry who said yes was:

Consumer products:	35 percent
Pharmaceuticals:	23 percent
Retailing:	20 percent
Banking:	15 percent
Computers:	15 percent

Given the emphasis placed on quality as a competitive necessity and the positive results achieved by the Japanese in quality manufacturing and service industries, such small numbers are appalling.

The First Quantum Power of Consciousness: Control Over Intention

We have 100 percent control over our intention. We can intend to lead, or not. Regardless of anything outside us, we own our intention without restriction, because intention resides in our consciousness. The full mastery of intention provides the initial spark of Quantum Leadership power.

Traditional science places power in forces and pressures

that operate on nature from the outside: pushing, pulling, lifting, restraining—forces that drive matter, material crushing against material to change its form.

Quantum physics reveals an inner power: the nonmaterial information-energy of consciousness. Intention is the first spark of consciousness that defines the Quantum Leader within. Intention indicates the seed of desire and the quality of regard. Quantum Leaders create their intention, and they have complete control over it. They consciously and willfully direct their intention to lead.

Not only do we have control over our intention, we are the only ones who know what it is. In my work with members of industry and government, I often hear people question the intention of others. Complaints about negative intentions are expressed with comments such as, "My boss is only in it for himself," "The people at the top don't care," or, "None of the political appointees wants to listen." I understand this frustration when I notice the accumulation of problems and the lack of forward movement in organizations. Some people do have negative intentions; bullies, tyrants, crooks, and liars do betray us. Yet no one really knows the intention of another. We evaluate intention by action, but intention is always hidden within.

Instead of speculating about the intentions of others, I suggest that people will better serve themselves, their company, and their country by clarifying their own intention. Each of us can decide at any moment what motivates us and what matters to us. We can consciously define our inner purpose and direct it toward progress. As American lawyer and writer Robert G. Ingersoll noted, "It is a blessed thing that in every age someone has had the individuality enough and courage enough to stand by his own convictions." Quantum Leaders spend their energy establishing their intention to lead. They direct their awareness toward attracting others to join them.

Action Idea: Join Dick's run. Make time each day, as Dick Frazar does on his daily run, to consider the structure of your intention. Determine what your intentions are, what they should be, and what they could be. This exercise requires exquisite sensitivity to the inner voice that defines who you are and what you can become. By making time to define your intention, you define the tenor and tone of that inner voice.

Action Idea: On-the-spot intention clarification. Define your specific intention before entering a situation. Ask yourself, "What is my intention in this situation?" You will know the answer once you reflect on it.

Action Idea: Focus your intention on leading. Intend to take the lead. Map the territory and chart a course in the leadership arena. Determine to focus on gaining willing followers. Then be intent on making it happen. This simple act of establishing your intention to lead empowers you to find the means to take action. Do not wait for others to be better leaders. Develop the leader within yourself.

Quantum Leader Attention

Attention reflects the design of intention. What you intend guides how you attend. Attention is the Quantum Leader's beam of consciousness directed outward toward the arena of possibilities and problems. The Quantum Paradigm explains that consciousness illuminates and creates reality. People move toward what they focus on. Thus, attention creates. What you put your attention on grows stronger in your life. What you pay *significant* attention to becomes your life.

Attention is generative, creating information for the future, and adaptive, relying on information for the moment. Kenneth W. Butterworth, Chairman of Loctite Corporation, directs his attention to the 95 percent of the world that does not live in the United States. As early as 1960, he began searching the globe for markets for Loctite's industrial adhesives and sealants. He continues to establish contacts and to set up future markets. In the summer of 1991, he traveled to Russia for ten days, with his attention guided by a "go-and-see" attitude. While he was aware that many shied away from the politically tumultuous and economically unstable countries of the former Soviet Union, Butterworth kept his attention open to it.

Bill Gates of Microsoft illustrates the power of attention turned way up high. Part of Gates's successful lead in the information processing industry is his in-depth knowledge of his company's products and the industry itself. Gates reads voraciously and devours detailed information. He recalls minor points from meetings held six months earlier, which even his product team often cannot remember. At Microsoft, this high-powered attention to detail has its own term in the company's lexicon: *granularity*.

Mastering the Quantum Leader within means paying attention to what is relevant. Quantum Leaders direct their beam of consciousness like an x-ray. They peer into a situation's inner workings and focus their consciousness like a probe, investigating and exploring for opportunities and ways to overcome problems. Quantum Leaders tune their senses to find and figure out the facts, and they snoop and search for signals to understand what is going on.

Motivated by his intention to lead, Dick Frazar turned the beam of his attention onto his new division. He spent several days at the division's offices, watching what was going on and talking to division members about their work. He commissioned a task force to investigate the group's operation and how it served its customers. He had an external consultant conduct in-depth, one-on-one interviews to explore issues with each division member. And he met with members of other divisions to determine their concerns. His attention power searched for possibilities and solutions to problems.

In the same way, the power of attention guided Sam Walton's now legendary practice of constantly traveling around the country and visiting each of his stores. Walton often drove his own car or piloted his private plane from one small town to the next, quizzing his employees for ideas, walking the aisles to assess the merchandise, and talking to customers about their likes and suggestions. Every Saturday starting at 3 A.M., he pored over weekly sales printouts searching for opportunities or trouble spots. He viewed these actions as the most important things he did.

Attention plays a vital role in today's economy. High-tech industries hope for dramatic productivity gains from AI—artificial intelligence—computerized equipment that mirrors human mental aptitudes and performs human tasks with lightning speed and complete efficiency. Quantum Leaders recognize that a similar kind of productivity can also increase through the power mastered through IA—increased attention.

Attention overcomes obstacles. During 1987 and 1988, John Lainhart, an inspector general for the U.S. government, focused his attention on improving security and operating system software for ten federal agency computer centers. These software packages disburse more than $273 billion annually to support primary federal agency missions. Lainhart's government-wide audit team was directed to assess the integrity of the federal computer system and to develop recommendations for improvements that affected computer system integrity.

The inspector general community traditionally avoided complicated system software assessments, believing that the technical complexities were too great and the necessary computer-assisted audit technologies were not available. But Lainhart never accepted this viewpoint. His intention was strong: Take the lead, tackle the problem, and make some progress.

Lainhart focused on how to do the job, not on why it could not be done. Several years earlier, he had developed a specialized software audit tool for the Department of Transportation. He thought that the same software could be modified and applied to other federal agencies.

Lainhart also directed his attention to overcoming the specific causes for hesitation in the inspector general community. He focused on several key issues: showing how to use the software in a well-planned manner, providing technical assistance on using the software, and demonstrating that the audit would result in significant dollar savings. Lainhart's attention paid off. All ten inspectors general signed on to the project, and the audit produced under Lainhart's leadership was hailed by the Computer Systems Security and Privacy Advisory Board, a panel of eminent public and private sector representatives, as one of the best pieces of computer security work ever done in the federal government.

The Second Quantum Power of Consciousness: Control Over Attention

Quantum Leaders understand that they control 100 percent of their attention power. Wherever they are, regardless of the circumstances, they can focus their attention in any direction or on any level of reality.

Classical physics confines attention to material reality. It gives power to what can be observed and measured with the five senses alone. With the classical physics mind-set, we remain isolated, separate from an objective world of matter.

But quantum physics shows us that attention is not dependent on matter. Rather, the power of consciousness serves as the creative element of the universe. We design the world and alter it by virtue of our attention.

The range of our attention power is defined by limits we impose on ourselves. If our limits are narrow, the seeds for trouble are sown. When General Motors ignored Japanese carmakers and instead focused all of its attention on Ford, Japan's share of the U.S. car market increased 10 percent from 1985 to 1991, while GM's market share decreased 7 percent. In the same way, CBS directed its attention to NBC and ABC and disregarded CNN, and Xerox used its attentional resources to worry about IBM and Kodak while Canon walked away with the copier business.

Failures of attention are avoidable because everyone has access to attention power and anyone can increase that power. Quantum Leaders consider: "What do I focus on during the day, and what do I let slip by?" "Whom do I talk to or ignore?" "Where do I go each day, and what areas do I rarely visit?"

"What do I read carefully, and what sources do I ignore?" "Whom do I listen to or shut out?" The answers to these questions reveal attention patterns, which Quantum Leaders can alter by opening themselves up to new avenues of information. In an exquisite state of heightened attention reinforced by the intention to lead, the Quantum Leader within can map the territory and chart a course in the leadership arena and gain followers.

> *Action Idea: Adopt a daily opportunity/problem search.* This action idea uses the concept "seek and you shall find." Allocate time each day to search for opportunities or solutions to problems. Look for ways to save a few moments on a work task or determine how your company can improve customer service, even if only in a small way.

> *Action Idea: Conduct an "attention analysis."* An "attention analysis" heightens awareness about a specific issue that requires some improvement. The analysis involves close scrutiny of a particular issue. For example, in the mid-1980s, Ray Alvord joined the Shell Oil Company's Organization Effectiveness and Training corporate office. Part of his mission was to upgrade the training programs offered to Shell managers. Alvord had a long history of adult education expertise in both the military and large corporations. He knew that video technology improved the presentation impact of training content and that it provided a powerful feedback tool for training participants engaged in role plays. Alvord conducted an attention analysis of the use of videos in Shell's existing training programs by scrutinizing the content of each course. To his surprise he found that only a few instructors used them. When Alvord restructured several courses to include video technology, the instructors and participants reported improvements in the programs.

> *Action Idea: Perform "AA" for 15 minutes a week.* This means that you amble aimlessly (AA) through your work-

place, keeping your attention open to new possibilities or previously unrecognized problems. Most people are extremely task focused at work, which can put blinders on their awareness. They rush from office to office and from meeting to meeting, or they move from one activity to another with their minds completely filled and unable to take in additional data. A high level of task focus can produce positive results (an attention analysis is an example of this type of behavior), but it can adversely narrow the scope of attention. By ambling aimlessly for a few minutes each week through your workplace, you take off the blinders of restricted attention and open your consciousness to new potentialities. Ambling aimlessly provides a time to stretch your mind so it can take in different configurations of information.

Quantum Leader Discrimination

Discrimination is the capacity to discern what is important. It maximizes available alternatives and determines how we interpret events. Quantum Leaders know that discrimination is essential in the risk-filled leadership arena, because judgment is paramount when no clear model or rule is available or when information is incomplete. Discrimination is also vital when attempting to influence diverse individuals to become willing followers.

One manager once remarked to me with no small amount of frustration in his voice, "Yeah, I know leadership requires judgment, but how do I make the right choices?" I understood how he felt, but I also recognized that his question reflected the classical physics worldview. The belief that the right choice can be known beforehand stems from the Newtonian paradigm that reality is deterministic and objective.

Quantum Leadership embraces the Heisenberg Uncertainty Principle, which indicates that it is impossible to know simultaneously both the position and the momentum of quantum particles. Werner Heisenberg, a pioneer in quantum physics, found that by observing a particle's position, its wavelike motion was suspended so that its speed could not be known. When the particle's wavelike momentum was observed, it became a blur and its position was lost. This paradoxical finding proved that we alter reality when we observe it. Heisenberg's finding was supposed to be meaningful only on the level of quantum particles. The Uncertainty Principle was not supposed to apply to large objects or ordinary events such as getting to work or directing a work group. However, it turns out that it does have relevance to the practical reality of leading.

Anyone who has grappled with leading realizes that there are no definitive markers sprinkled along the path to serve as a guide through the uncertain leadership wilderness. Uncertainty of outcomes dominates the leadership arena. Leaders are expected to guide, but paradoxically, they can never be sure where they are going. Quantum Leaders map the territory by *discovering* ways to exploit possibilities and overcome obstacles. They chart a course by figuring out where to go and how to gain followers—efforts that are always fraught with uncertainty.

Quantum physics reveals that leadership uncertainty extends beyond the problem of not knowing *the* outcome of a course of action to include the uncertainty that any action can have objective meaning. Just as the act of observation creates either the particle or the wave, Quantum Leadership indicates that the meaning the leader assigns to events depends on what the leader *chooses to observe* and how he or she *chooses to interpret* the environment. The discrimination of the Quantum Leader within, consciousness, creates meaning.

Discrimination, as it is defined here, goes beyond the findings of psychological studies of perception that suggest that people often distort what they see, using selective perception to notice only certain events or relying on stereotypes to evaluate people and situations. Implicit within such studies is the belief that we *mistakenly* interpret events—that is, it is assumed that an objective reality exists but we simply do not recognize it or else fail to understand it accurately. But quantum physics shows that reality depends on the observer's consciousness. Quantum Leaders recognize that consciousness unfolds through intention and attention and is directed by discrimination that creates the meaning of reality for the observer.

Dick Frazar's discrimination clarified his approach to the problematic division. As a result of his highly focused attention, Dick discovered several possibilities for action: (1) The division could be eliminated and the work outsourced; (2) massive changes in the division's personnel could be made (through firing or transferring some people) in an effort to modify the group's disruptive behavior patterns; or (3) Dick could challenge the group to reinvent itself and provide his support for this effort. Each choice had its pluses and minuses.

Dick chose the third option: working with the group to bring about needed changes. He attributed the group's problems to a lack of support from previous management. He also believed that several individuals within the group truly wanted to change. Dick felt that his support would show the group that he wanted to empower them, which would send a powerful and positive message to other managers about how to maximize the organization's human capital. These interpretations were created in Dick's consciousness, within his locus of discrimination. Others in the company preferred to disband the division or fire certain personnel because of the different meanings they assigned to information about the division.

Dick commissioned an external consultant to conduct a two-day team-building retreat in a well-appointed resort hotel, to send a message to the group that they deserved a positive environment in which to work on issues. While the group was away, he personally answered the busy telephones to cover their work activity, thus letting them know he would support them in every way he could. When the team-building retreat was over, Dick contracted for a one-day conflict management training program to help the group overcome problems handling differences. He wanted them to know that he believed in collaboration over destructive competition as the approach to resolve problems. Dick also convinced the other divisions to participate in a customer service audit of his division. He believed his division members needed to understand how others viewed them, and he was convinced that they would assist their internal customers better if they were given specific suggestions for change.

These particular choices reveal Dick's use of discrimination—the choices he made and the meaning he assigned to reality. In contrast, another manager criticized Dick for his choices, despite their positive impact.

The Quantum Leader within creates the path while also traveling along it by consciously discriminating. Quantum Leaders maximize and assign meaning to choices that provide opportunities for overcoming obstacles. Sam Walton continually looked for ways to attract more customer loyalty and help his employees organize for greater success. Therefore, he spent hours visiting his stores, gathering as much information as he could and being as aware as possible. In contrast, former RJR Nabisco CEO Lou Gerstner admitted that the company blundered in 1992 by ignoring choices about consumer product demand for low-priced, generic cigarettes. RJR Nabisco had pumped most of its $2.5 billion marketing budget into its high-priced cigarette brands, while Phillip Morris and England's BAT Industries flooded the market with cheap alternatives. Industry volume for plain-wrapped cigarettes ballooned to 10 percent, but RJR failed to interpret this information as meaningful.

The Third Quantum Power of Consciousness: Control Over Discrimination

Quantum Leaders know that they have 100 percent control over their discrimination. They accept responsibility for what happens to them because they determine the meaning of what happens. Because they can choose what to observe and can create alternative possibilities for interpreting what they observe, they know that all potentials exist. Quantum Leaders continually generate choices to create multiple options in order to uncover as many possibilities as they can. This requires having the intention to do so and keeping attention power focused. You have probably heard statements such as, "That's it! I don't want to talk about it any more!" or, "No, there's no use considering this any further!" Such declarations reveal that consciousness has shut down and discrimination has halted.

To interpret every possibility in the most useful manner, Quantum Leaders also keep consciousness flexible. Nordstrom, the highly successful, Seattle-based retailer with sales of $3.4 billion in 1993, has formalized this notion for its employees. Its entire employee policy manual consists of one sentence: "Use your best judgment at all times." Keeping consciousness flexible means being aware of the framework or meaning assigned to choices and consciously reframing the choices to create meanings that inspire action and motivate others to follow. This also demands the intention to be flexible and adapting attention to take in new data. The components of the Quantum Leadership model—mapping the territory and charting a course to perceive what others don't and going into the G.A.P.—are the processes Quantum Leaders use to keep consciousness moving and flexible.

With 100 percent control over discrimination, Quantum Leaders know that it is better *not* to decide until they have to. They seek additional information and evaluate possibilities, and they do not make up their minds (which usually means closing the mind down) until they are required to make a choice. Ultimately, of course, a choice for action must be made, at which time they find that time and space boundaries limit the range of choices that can be developed: Deadlines must be met, resources are limited, and important information may not be available. Intention, attention, and discrimination guide the Quantum Leader within to take initiative.

> *Action Idea: Allow options.* Over the next few weeks, give each person you work with the opportunity to develop at least one alternative option for a decision. More choices keep consciousness moving; the more choices there are, the more possibility there is for better choices, which increases discriminatory capacity.

Action Idea: Generate five additional choices. When people find the "right answer," consciousness stops moving, and during idea generation, most people limit their options by favoring a particular choice too quickly. Therefore, to keep consciousness lively, make it a practice to generate five (or more) additional choices *after* you believe you have made a really good one.

Action Idea: Change the meaning. After you have thought through and interpreted a situation, spend a few minutes considering how the information you have could mean something different. Change the meaning to try and make it more productive, more inspiring, or more interesting.

Quantum Leader Initiative

Initiative means action. As Napoleon said, "Take time to deliberate, but when the time for action has arrived, stop thinking and go in." And as Ralph Waldo Emerson said, "Good thoughts are no better than good dreams unless they are expressed."

Yasutsugu Takeda's initiative helped create Hitachi's flourishing optoelectronics business because he took action by working with semiconductor lasers. When Takeda first arrived at the company's research labs in 1970, he could not interest any Hitachi factory in commercializing semiconductor lasers because the lasers were hard to fabricate. General Electric, which had invented them, had backed out of the area precisely because of these fabrication problems. Yet Takeda was unwilling to be derailed by others' disappointments. He wrote up a catalog of semiconductor lasers he could custom-produce at his workbench and mailed copies to IBM, Bell Telephone, Xerox, and Canon, which placed orders for the lasers. Armed with the orders, Takeda persuaded the head of one of the Hitachi chip production plants to begin manufacture. By 1992, Hitachi had cornered 60 percent of the world's market for the special laser devices now used by AT&T and others in their transcontinental fiberoptic telephone networks.

The opposite of initiative is to sit around thinking about what to do without taking action. Inaction, despite the best intentions, attention, and discrimination, foretells failure for those who would otherwise lead. Or as the saying goes, "He who hesitates is lunch!"

In a July 1990 column written for *U.S. News and World Report* just after George Bush approved a tax hike, political consultant David Gergan noted that the public would never forget how cynically Bush had spoken as a candidate when he invited Americans to "read my lips." But, Gergan argued, people would forgive Bush if he acted courageously. He suggested that if Bush took the necessary steps to wrap up an agreement and solve the budget problem once and for all, he would be exonerated. Gergan called it "a defining moment." Yet Bush failed to take action in response to that moment. Instead, he blamed Congress as an unwilling player in the budget morass. Inaction on the domestic economic front plagued Bush throughout the remainder of his presidency. On November 3, 1992, the voters refused to follow him for four more years.

Initiative drives Quantum Leaders to map the territory and chart a course to perceive what others don't, and to perform enlightened action to gain follower commitment. Initiative is the end product of intention, attention, and discrimination. The Quantum Leader within formulates action based on these other three components of consciousness. Initiative curves back through consciousness and motivates the leader within to recommit the intention to lead. Initiative refocuses attention on possibilities and solutions. It refines discrimination to develop more choices and to assign meanings that inspire and motivate.

The internal work Dick Frazar did during his daily run paid off for his new division. His intention to make a difference, the hours of attention he devoted to understanding the situation, and his discriminating interpretation of choices translated into successful action. The resulting team-building and conflict-management interventions he instituted caused key changes within his division. Division members restructured job assignments to even out the work load. A weekly staff discussion meeting, initiated to improve internal communication, caused differences to be surfaced more easily and problem resolution to tend more toward win-win solutions. The customer service audit resulted in more open and positive lines of communication between the division and its internal customers, and a cross-functional learning effort was introduced so that all groups could better understand each others' procedures and thereby be more responsive to each others' work demands. The division members' surly attitudes softened as they came to understand and appreciate the needs and expectations of other departments. Work efficiency increased and staff morale improved.

The Fourth Quantum Power of Consciousness: The Nike Effect

Quantum Leaders recognize that life has limits, that action always involves risk, and that they cannot do everything. But they also embrace the idea that they can always do *something*, because they know they have 100 percent control over their initiative.

The science fiction film *Aliens* depicts a commando group sent into space to investigate a story about the strange alien force found during an initial mission. In one scene, Ripley, who was part of the first mission, and an inexperienced officer in charge of the group observe the commandos on special video equipment as the group reconnoiters the deserted facility in which the alien creature lives. When the commandoes come under a brutal attack by the alien, chaos reigns. Under severe threat, they need direction from their young officer, but, paralyzed by fear and confusion, he is incapable of offering meaningful guidance. Ripley shouts at the officer, "Do something, do something," but he remains frozen. Finally, Ripley leaps forward and drives into the facility, rescuing the besieged commandoes.

Ripley's dramatic action illustrates that the Quantum Leader within wears Nike running shoes and is willing to "Just Do It!" The Quantum Leader's consciousness is outfitted with mental Nikes that help him or her take the necessary leap of leadership.

> *Action Idea: Resolve to take the "risk of initiative" at least once a day.* Each day, resolve to take some initiative to overcome a problem, exploit a possibility, and take the lead. Move. Act. Your action will not always result in gaining willing followers, and even if it does, you might not always lead them toward a successful outcome. Initiative involves a risk, but do not be fearlessly foolish. Take reasonable risks. But take some action.

Neuharth's Newspaper: A Feature Story on the Leader Within

It took *The Wall Street Journal* seventy-seven years to reach a circulation of 1 million readers. *USA Today* did it in just one year. In just seven years after its inception, with almost 4.8 million readers, "McPaper," as *USA Today* has been labeled, became the number one daily in the United States.

The dramatic impact of *USA Today* originated in the consciousness of Al Neuharth, its founder and father. From the time he joined the newspaper business in the 1950s in South Dakota, Neuharth carried in his mind the idea of a national daily newspaper. His intention stayed with him throughout his climb to the top of the Gannett publishing empire.

Neuharth's purpose, says Peter Pritchard in *The Making of McPaper*, was to create a different kind of news daily. Not only would it be national in scope, it would be, in Neuharth's words, "enlightening and enjoyable to the nation's readers; informative and impelling to the nation's leaders; challenging and competitive to the nation's journalists; refreshing and rewarding to the nation's advertisers." He wanted *USA Today* to "serve as a forum for better understanding and unity to make the USA truly one nation."

Once the paper was launched, Neuharth focused his attention on creating the unique format that today jumps out from its TV look-alike racks. Neuharth had the paper on his mind when he jogged each day, during meeting breaks, and as he criss-crossed the country in the corporate jet. He spent hours person-ally checking *USA Today* paper racks in different cities. As he jogged past racks, he would check to make sure that they were filled with papers. Obsessed with quality, he sometimes drove from rack to rack in a limo, his pockets bulging with quarters, assessing an issue's color, format, and "feel." In the October 15, 1982, Rochester, New York, edition, Neuharth noticed that the sky on the weather map was purple. He wrote a note to *USA Today* President Phil Gialanella: "Skies are basically blue. What happened?"

Thousands of choices were considered as the paper devel-oped. Sometimes Neuharth's judgments were winners, such as the use of color photos—especially the full-page color weather maps, the state-by-state news briefs, and the extensive sports statistics. At others, his discrimination resulted in major mis-takes. He ignored the mail delivery and home subscription mar-ket. Why? Neuharth's discrimination told him, *Think single-copy sales*, which limited the meaningful possibilities of other distri-bution channels. He purchased a computer system that turned out to be too small to handle the paper's changing and expand-ing needs, including the huge volume of home subscriptions the paper eventually had.

USA Today has had its critics. It has been denounced as "junk-food journalism, tasty but without substance." The paper lost money for several years, something that Neuharth expected and was willing to accept. His intention included a long-term view rather than the typical limited sight that pursues short-term profits. Despite its detractors, no one can denounce the im-pact of Neuharth's newspaper, nor can anyone deny that the paper has a loyal readership. Many have followed the lead that began and blossomed in Al Neuharth's consciousness.

6

Map the Territory and Chart a Course: Perceive What Others Don't

"We all live under the same sky, but we don't all have the same horizon."

—Konrad Adenauer, West Germany's chancellor, 1949–1963

Ron Fisher walked out of the hotel into the blazing Dallas sunlight. He needed a break to think through all the information he had heard during the morning's meetings. It was March 1990, and Fisher, a senior researcher at the U.S. Department of Transportation, was participating in a national workshop, sponsored by the Federal Highway Administration. The gathered group of industry, government, and academic community experts, informally called Mobility 2000, focused on improving highway transportation through rapidly advancing electronics and communications technologies.

As Fisher walked, the sun's brilliance seemed to help him perceive that the meeting participants were overlooking a critical issue. The workshop had focused almost entirely on ways advanced information technologies could improve private automobile transportation. Fisher, however, believed that more private auto usage, no matter how technologically sophisticated it might become, would increase pollution, continue to deplete energy resources, and probably create more highway congestion. He recognized that the proposed Mobility 2000 agenda needed to include an additional effort: to improve public transportation usage and increase the development of various ride-sharing choices.

When Fisher returned to Washington, he convinced his agency's head, Brian Clymer, that his vision was worth following. And in May, at a national meeting to review the Mobility 2000 effort, Fisher got Clymer on the program to promote the inclusion of public transportation on the Mobility 2000 agenda and gained a solid base of support. When, as a result of this summit, the Intelligent Vehicle Highway Society America (IVHS) was formed, Fisher, building on the support Clymer had established, convinced key leaders to add a new committee, the Advanced Public Transportation System, to the initial IVHS committee structure. Public transit is now fully integrated into the mainstream effort of the national IVHS program.

Moving Consciousness Into the Leadership Arena

The Quantum Leadership model indicates that Quantum Leaders interact with the leadership arena when they map the territory, to recognize possibilities or problems, and chart a course, to provide a direction that takes advantage of opportunities or overcomes obstacles (Figure 6-1). These are the processes Quantum Leaders execute when they operate beyond the boundaries of organizationally prescribed action *(the fifth natural law of leadership)*.

A Road Less Traveled

A simple metaphor explains the process of mapping the territory and charting a course. Picture a road, and imagine that it repre-

Figure 6-1. The Quantum Leadership model: The leadership arena.

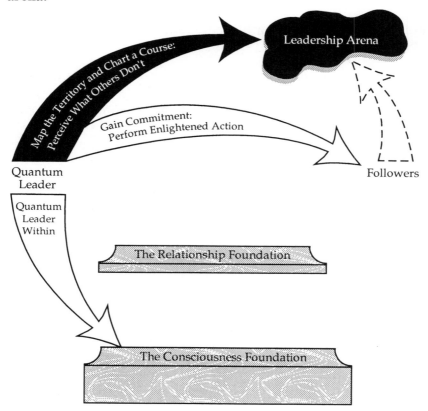

sents an organization's established pathway and procedures prescribed to achieve goals or accomplish an agenda. For example, the road could represent the path established to achieve a corporation's strategy, or symbolize the established procedures of a company's manufacturing procedures or employee benefits system. The road could even portray the prescribed guidelines that govern a small-group meeting, such as a voting system to make decisions. In all of these cases, the road defines the existing system, and it is paved with strategies, plans, structures, rules, regulations, policies, and procedures (Figure 6-2).

In the road metaphor, managers, or anyone else in positions of formal authority, are responsible for moving the organization or group along the road. They carry out the plan set by the system and ensure that others comply with the rules, regulations, policies, and procedures. Managers who move straight down the center of the road in double-time are typically considered very successful. Such individuals, labeled the fast trackers, move ahead with unswerving energy. Yet even those who plod along, weaving their way ever so slowly forward, usually reap rewards as long as they continue to make progress along the pathway.

When the road adequately enables people to get where they need to go, managerial expertise and formal authority can effectively guide and direct work and successfully enable the organization to accomplish its goals. The prescribed path suffices when people know what to do.

Now imagine a deep rut in the road or an obstacle across it (Figure 6-3). The rut causes people or an entire organization to get stuck. It could be a destructive flare-up between members of

Figure 6-2. Established organizational pathway.

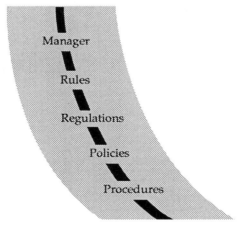

Manager

Rules

Regulations

Policies

Procedures

Figure 6-3. Obstacles, ruts, and opportunities along the road.

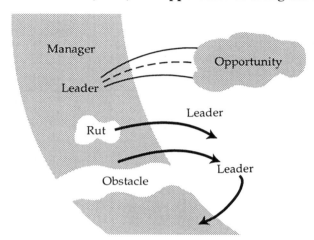

a diverse work group, which limits their ability to communicate; a set of group norms that restrict an organization's ability to take risks; or even an organization-wide penchant for conducting endless rounds of meetings to make a single decision. An obstacle is a barrier that blocks the way—perhaps a competitor's unforeseen new product that steals an organization's market share, or an unexpected equipment breakdown that halts a production line. If the established rules and regulations offer no method to get people out of the rut, they remain confined. If the established pathway provides no means to get past the unexpected problem represented by the roadblock, no progress can be made.

Now imagine that an opportunity exists off the established pathway: maybe a new market, a new technology, a new method for designing work processes, or a new approach to evaluating employees. If the established procedures provide no means to create a new path, the means to exploit the opportunity do not exist.

In each of these cases, Quantum Leaders are needed to identify the road less traveled by mapping the territory; they must understand ruts, identify obstacles, and recognize opportunities.

Then they can chart a course by helping people out of ruts, directing them around or through obstacles, or establishing a new path to take advantage of opportunities.

In 1990, *Fortune* magazine reported how Richard Miller, CEO of the computer company Wang, recognized how a leader helps a company get around a roadblock. One of his managers had discovered that customers had serious complaints about Wang's quality of service and suggested resolving the problem by giving customers who purchased certain computers a fax machine to gain easy access to Wang for service questions. Furthermore, the manager proposed that the free fax should include a number customers could use to fax messages directly to Miller's desk. Miller accepted the idea and commented, "In my book, that's leadership."

An example of getting out of a rut occurred during an organization's newly formed strategic planning task force meeting regarding the voting procedures it would use to make decisions. The organization was composed of three groups, which had always operated autonomously. The goal now was to integrate the organization into a more coherent whole. The task force had a proportionate number of members from each area: One area had five representatives, another had eight representatives, and eleven people represented the third.

Over the two days of its initial task force meeting, the group spent nearly four hours discussing how it would make decisions, and sometimes the debate got heated. When members of one area proposed what it considered an ideal decision-making method, members of the two others, fearful that they were not fairly represented by that method, objected. Various points of view were debated, and numerous examples of the pros and cons of different decision rules were suggested. But the rut kept getting deeper as the group seemed incapable of agreeing on how it would decide issues.

Finally, a woman who had been silent during these discussions explained that the group members from each of the three areas obviously did not trust members from the other two areas. She indicated that this was understandable since most of them had not worked together before. She thought that trust would come as they worked together. She also pointed out that part of their charge was to develop an integrated organizational strategy, which would blur the existing autonomous operating lines. Therefore, the task force members had to start thinking as representatives of the entire organization, not as delegates from their separate areas. Her comments catalyzed the group, and they agreed on a decision-making method. The woman got the task force out of a rut and back on track.

Robert Epstein, who cofounded the computer company Sybase, one of *Fortune* magazine's 1992 fastest-growing companies, illustrates mapping the territory and charting a course to exploit opportunities. Epstein explained that "an established company's major goal is to defend what it did last year. That's the fatal flaw." Epstein broke that boundary with an opportunistic consciousness, which drove Sybase to create software for the new computer networking trend. Bigger computer companies, entrenched in existing procedures, did not see the network trend coming.

Quantum Leaders also map the territory and chart a course to reengineer an organization's path. For example, Aetna Life & Casualty improved its process for serving customers whose cars were stolen. It reduced the claim time from a system that used to take between two and five days to a single telephone call to an 800 number that provides all-in-one service, such as where to pick up a rental car, the name of the agent who will handle the claim, and an appointment date. Aetna CEO Ronald Compton told *Fortune* magazine that he expects to save $100 million annually from this reengineering effort.

The Beginner's Mind

Mapping the territory and charting a course occurs when the Quantum Leader's consciousness perceives what others don't, which means he or she has a unique insight into the uncertainty of the leadership arena. The importance of perceiving what others don't while mapping the territory and charting a course can be illustrated by picturing a group of people trapped in a burning room. If a pathway to safety is clearly evident, the people will not need someone to lead them. They can lead themselves. But if no visible way to safety is clear and no one seems to know what to do, someone has to take the lead. If a voice cries out, "Here, we can escape this way. Follow me!" and the group responds by committing to this directive, that person has perceived what others did not and gained followers.

Quantum Leaders have what Zen masters describe as the "beginner's mind"—a mind open to possibilities rather than an awareness filled with limiting beliefs, restrictive bias, and faulty assumptions. The Quantum Leader's consciousness moves to identify deeper layers of order and possibilities where others observe only chaos or fail to recognize new choices.

Quantum Leaders know that to foresee something creates it. Ron Fisher foresaw the need for public transit to be part of a federal program to improve transportation; as a result, the Advanced Public Transit System was created. The Wang manager perceived a unique method to ensure customers' of the company's positive commitment to customer service. The woman in the strategic task force perceived that the group members would learn to trust each other and that they had to think as a unified organization. And Robert Epstein perceived the network trend while others did not.

Perceiving what others don't involves thinking the unthinkable to find and create the future. Observers marveled at Walt Disney's ability to "see beneath the surface" and visualize possibilities. He pictured the magic and grandeur of Disneyworld in the undeveloped central Florida marshes.

Perceiving what others don't can have a dramatic impact. In *The Crisis Years*, Michael Bechloss describes an incident that occurred during the 1962 Cuban Missile crisis. At the height of tension, President Kennedy received a letter from Soviet Premier Khrushchev that was an impassioned plea for peace worded in a conciliatory tone. Khrushchev seemed to be saying the Soviets would, without conditions, meet the president's demands to withdraw the offensive missiles that U.S. spy planes had discovered in Cuba. Kennedy was elated—until twelve hours later when a second letter arrived that sounded more belligerent. Now Khrushchev demanded concessions: In return for the removal of missiles from Cuba, the United States would have to dismantle its own missile sites in Turkey.

Kennedy was both furious and stumped. Why the second letter? What did it mean? And he and his advisers had a deeper, more distressing suspicion: The language of the second communication did not sound like Khrushchev. What was going on in the halls of the Kremlin? Had the Soviet Central Committee ousted its premier? Was the military now in charge? How should the United States respond to the contradictory letters?

Kennedy gripped the two letters while he and his closest advisers anxiously considered their dilemma. McGeorge Bundy perceived a breathtakingly simple but ingenious solution: Simply ignore the second letter and respond to the first. Bundy reasoned that the first letter provided an offer the president could accept. Kennedy stopped in amazement. The idea was brilliant; it could work. He immediately directed Bundy, Attorney General Robert Kennedy, and Ted Sorenson, a key adviser, to draft a reply to the first letter.

The ploy worked. Khrushchev commanded the Soviet ships en route to Cuba to turn back. He ordered the dismantling of those missile sites already in place and the removal of all offensive missile equipment from Cuba. The Cuban missile crisis was over.

Quantum Leadership begins when consciousness moves. The classical physics mind-set created the belief that leadership begins with the visible, material reality of action. Quantum physics reveals that the actual starting point for leadership exists in consciousness.

The Components of the Quantum Leader's Consciousness

Mapping the territory and charting a course has two components: vision and conscious observation. Quantum Leader consciousness perceives what others don't by moving in either or both of these directions to reveal possibilities or uncover problems.

Quantum Leader Vision

Vision is perhaps the most popular buzzword heard today in discussions of leadership and management. In my consulting work, when managers describe what it takes to be a leader, I continually hear the statement, "The leader must have vision."

Vision is the Quantum Leader's unique wide-angle and long-range lens of awareness. Vision enables the leader to see into the future and to comprehend big picture possibilities. With this focus of consciousness, the leader perceives an attractive and credible future state.

Limited vision forecloses possibilities. In 1895, Lord Kelvin, president of the Royal Society, said, "Heavier than air flying machines are impossible." In 1899, the director of the U.S. Patent Office proclaimed, "Everything that can be invented, has been invented." In 1927, Harry Warner, head of Warner Bros. Pictures, responding to the advent of talking pictures, snapped, "Who the hell wants to hear actors talk!"

A limited vision can foretell serious problems for a company. IBM could not see over the horizon when it chose to place an Intel Corp. microchip and use Microsoft Corp. operating software in its PCs. IBM's move allowed these two companies to become industry giants, and it enabled anyone to get into the computer business and clone IBM machines. Had IBM executives perceived with a wider-angle, longer-term view, they might have purchased the technologies from these companies. Perceptual blinders also stunned Digital Equipment. In 1975, Ken Olsen, Digital's dynamic and intelligent founder, argued, "Nobody is going to want a computer in their house," and decided to ignore the burgeoning PC market in favor of mainframes. The outcome was huge financial losses for Digital.

Failures of vision might explain a rash of CEO firings that swept across many organizations in the early 1990s: James Robinson III, discredited by American Express; Tom Barrett, wheeled out by Goodyear; James Ketelsen, drummed out by Tenneco; and Rod Canion, deleted by Compaq. In each case, the boards of directors sensed that a new eye was needed to perceive their company's future. When Eastman Kodak's CEO, Kay R. Whitmore, was moved out of the picture in August 1993, the company's announcement that it would look for an outsider to replace him conveyed a clear message: A fresh perspective was needed. Only a new focus of consciousness could perceive ways to tackle the changing environment. With vision, Quantum Leaders map the territory to recognize the shape of the horizon and then chart a course to get there.

Map the Territory: Develop Vision

Quantum Leaders map the territory to create a vision of what their organizations could be. Quantum Leaders focus their wide-angle, long-range lens of awareness on the organization's potential future.

Action Idea: Identify an ideal future state. Focus your Quantum Leader-as-perceiver consciousness on what your organization could become in its industry or in related industries. JVC imagined a VCR sitting in every home; Motorola wants to place a hand-held personal communicator in your pocket. Defining what you want to become maps the territory of the uncreated future. Spend time each week imagining possible futures for your organization. Ask yourself, "If the company could be anything it wanted to be, and do it well, what would we be?"

Action Idea: Identify core competencies. What skills and technologies does your organization need to achieve your ideal future state? What will your organization have to do to provide customer benefits in unique ways that will distinguish it in the future? Federal Express founder Fred Smith had a vision of overnight package delivery. He foresaw the need to develop competencies in bar-code technology, wireless communication, and network management.

Action Idea: Conduct a "Niagara analysis." If you found yourself in a boat heading for a plunge over Niagara Falls, you would have to make some fast decisions to change course. A Niagara analysis means you ask yourself: "Will the organization's existing strategy and competencies take it to the ideal future state, or will we plummet over the falls?" The previous two action ideas move your consciousness to perceive where you want to be and the resources you need to get there; the Niagara analysis brings the future and present face to face to evaluate what you have to do to get where you want to go.

Ron Fisher's story offers a glimpse into how the Quantum Leader-as-perceiver uses these first three action ideas:

1. He perceived an ideal future: technological innovation and reduced pollution, less traffic congestion, and improved energy usage.
2. He identified the Department of Transportation's core competencies before he arrived in Dallas.
3. He conducted a Niagara analysis, which revealed a flaw that others did not recognize. He perceived the potential problems regarding an overemphasis on upgrading only private transportation methods, which prompted him to focus on integrating public transit into the overall effort.

Ken Auletta, in a 1993 article for *The New Yorker*, describes Barry Diller's vision. Diller, who heads shop-at-home TV network QVC, has visitation rites in most living rooms today because of that vision. In 1992, Diller quit Fox Inc., the network he helped build into the fourth major TV power, and began looking into the world of global communications by studying the key communications industries: TV networks, cable companies, telephone companies, computer companies, consumer electronics companies, and publishers.

For several months, Diller mapped the territory with focused attention on components of a world previously unknown to him. He researched digital-compression technology, fiber-optic cables, computer equipment, and computer services like Prodigy and interactive TV. And everything new he encountered made him think in new ways. He perceived a "communications enabler" that would sit next to a TV set and provide an interactive format to offer consumers any form of information or entertainment they wanted. The television would be transformed into an input-output device with a computer remote like a computer mouse. Diller perceived that TV cable systems would lead the way into the information future. He had learned that 63 percent of all American homes were already wired for cable. Furthermore, when Diller met with cable people, he was impressed by their lively, inquisitive nature and by the way they treated technology as an ally.

Diller hit upon QVC, the home shopping network, which he saw as a powerhouse for the future to realize his vision in the world of interactive media. In its first twenty months of operation, QVC earned nearly $56 million. Diller perceived QVC as a vehicle—the springboard to a universe beyond the limited world of TV channels, an interactive information services medium. He became a partner and CEO of QVC.

> *Action Idea: Map your industry.* Identify the key competitors you expect to face in the future based on your current industry rivals. Specify industry strengths and weaknesses in comparison to your organization. Be ruthless; this is not the time for wishful thinking or vain comparisons that diminish the capacities of your rivals. Your vision must not be blurred with overly optimistic forecasts.
>
> *Action Idea: Map the global landscape.* Specify factors from the larger global landscape that might have an impact on your organization. (Think big.) What technological trends

could reshape or completely redefine your industry? Do not ignore industries or social/political forces that appear to be tangential. In a global competitive environment, everything can affect everything else. Negotiations between Denmark and other European nations regarding the formation of the European Community seemed far removed from store sales at Fiesta, a Houston-based grocery chain. Yet the European Community bargaining led to a resolution regarding import restrictions on apples grown in Denmark, which affected Fiesta's produce offerings. Map the global landscape to increase your awareness of any second- or third-order influences on your organization's long-term behavior.

Action Idea: Perform a stakeholder appraisal. List the key constituents your organization has to serve to survive today. Then list those whom you might serve in your desired future. Include any persons, groups, or institutions that can exert influence on your organization or that your organization strongly influences. Specify their interests, priorities, and expectations. Identify the potential opportunities and threats stakeholders pose to your company now and in the future.

The three previous action ideas help clarify the forces you will face as you chart a course to move toward your vision.

Chart a Course: Propose a Vision

Mapping the territory with vision provides a picture of the unknown future across a wide landscape. Quantum Leaders-as-perceivers then direct consciousness to chart a course and define or redefine how to get where they want to go.

Action Idea: Attend a future world screening. Imagine that you have the chance to attend a unique cinema that shows films from the future. In the future world cinema, your company achieves your vision. What makes your company successful in this future world? How did your organization get to this place? Be flexible and speculative in your answers, since many possibilities could explain this future reality. Consider how far into the future your film projected. Should you extend the time frame because your horizon is too close? If your perception is too vague, should you draw it back to clarify the path? Now focus on the details that defined your success. What technologies, customers and their needs, or competitive realities exist that your company exploited to get ahead?

Action Idea: Produce your own movie. What should your organization begin to do differently now to realize the success you saw in the future world cinema? Chart a course with any and all possibilities that could work. What do your organization and its members have to learn now to compete? How does your organization develop or acquire the necessary technologies? Create several versions of a movie that portrays how your organization succeeds. Cut and edit your script to determine which picture gives you the most useful course.

Quantum Leader Conscious Observation

A friend once told me, "God is in the details." I also heard from someone else that "the devil is in the details." I am not sure which of these statements is true, yet both make it clear that a conscious awareness of the details is important to some pretty powerful folks.

The second way Quantum Leaders map the territory and chart a course is through conscious observation. Using a zoom-lens focus, they map the territory of possibilities that affect the present and more immediate future, and they chart a course to overcome problems and exploit current opportunities. Conscious observers pay attention to the day-to-day, hour-to-hour, minute-to-minute realities that make up most people's daily work routine.

Conscious observers "look at the company, not at the paper," as Tom Watson, founder of IBM, described it. They go into the trenches to study, stare, and scrutinize what is going on. In 1970, Robert Townsend explained the need to get out of the office and observe his company's operation. After one year as head of rental car company Avis, Townsend turned the company around from drowning in red ink to a highly profitable balance sheet. In *Up the Organization,* Townsend credits much of his success to the time he spent out of the executive suite and in the trenches with the employees and customers.

William Malec, chief financial officer of the Tennessee Valley Authority (TVA), practices conscious observation one day each month when he spends time doing the job of a TVA employee. Malec might scrub toilets at midnight, sort mail at 5:00 A.M., punch in data for the purchasing clerk, or perform any one of the other jobs held by the 2,000 employees at the TVA facilities in Muscle Shoals, Alabama, Knoxville, or Chattanooga, Tennessee. Malec explained his motivation to *Forbes* magazine: "When you get down into their jobs, they will tell you things you normally don't hear."

Henry Schinberg, president and chief operating officer of Johnston Coca-Cola Bottling Group of Chattanooga, Coke's number 2 bottler, is also an astute conscious observer. Schinberg spends 80 percent of his time in the field, meeting with retailers and visiting Johnston's sixty-five plants and distribution centers scattered throughout the Midwest. The computer terminal on his desk pumps out details that Schinberg drinks up ravenously. As he told *Fortune* writer Patricia Sellers, "I can tell you how much of each brand we sold yesterday in any city and the average discount and the profit margins."

King Henry V wandered from campfire to campfire, chatting with the soldiers on the eve of the Battle of Agincourt. Jack Welch, CEO of General Electric, makes time each month to go to Crotonville, GE's management development center, to meet directly with managers attending courses and answer their questions.

Conscious observation is the quantum power of attention power turned up to high. It is a requirement of those at all organizational levels who have the intention to lead. Conscious observation may seem like a commonsense behavior, but many organizations have suffered when consciousness failed to zoom in and respond to critical details. Consider the Pinkerton Agency, America's first private detective firm. Pinkerton's logo of the unblinking eye and its motto, "We never sleep," helped it become the largest, most revered security company in the country. Yet in 1988 Pinkerton's stellar reputation was severely tarnished, and the company was bleeding money; the nuclear security division alone was losing $2 million a year. Some regional offices employed twenty people when only two were needed. Other branches were supposed to have entire fleets of automobiles, but no one could locate them. Still other branches had 120-day-old receivables with nobody out trying to collect them. It would not take Sherlock Holmes to recognize these elementary clues, described by S. Greengard in *American Way* magazine. Someone at Pinkerton must have been asleep to overlook such problems.

Here is a simple test to challenge your abilities as a conscious observer. Count the number of *f*'s in the following:

> Count the F's
> Feature films are the re-
> sult of years of scienti-
> fic study combined with
> the experience of years.

How many did you get? Four, five, six, seven? Count again if you did not find seven. Notice which you missed. People usually overlook the small details—the *f* in the word *of*—or simply do not consider certain information—the *f* in the title.

Map the Territory: Develop Conscious Observation

Quantum Leaders map the territory with conscious observation to identify more immediate and localized opportunities and problems.

Action Idea: Watch the message board. Imagine your organization is a message board continually blinking with information about opportunities and solutions to problems that people might typically miss. "Watch the message board" means spending time each day consciously focused on any signals or cues and then using your discrimination to determine their meaning. You already have significant experience in message board responsiveness. Consider how you react to your ringing telephone, e-mail, the blinking light on your answering machine, or the beeping sound from your microwave oven. Most people jump to acknowledge these messages, but they turn off their homing device of consciousness to a myriad of other messages blinking, beeping, flashing, and ringing all around them. Use the same receptivity to traditional message indicators when you watch the entire organization as a message board

Action Idea: Get your head above the grass. Lyndon Johnson warned that we have to "stop keeping our heads below the grass." Lift your head to observe, study, scrutinize, and notice the events around you. There is safety below the grass, but you cannot perceive how to take the lead from that posture.

Action Idea: Place the Pala bird on your shoulder. In the Nobel Prize–winning novel *Island,* Aldous Huxley described Pala, a mythical paradise in which a strange black bird flew about squawking in a high, nasal monotone the phrases, "Attention, Attention" and "Here and now, here and now." Place an imaginary bird on your shoulder to let its call remind you to observe. Focus your attention power, and maintain your awareness on the messages of the present.

Action Idea: Remember the Challenger. Warning messages were sent about the faulty seals on the *Challenger* space shuttle in 1985, but those messages were ignored in favor of other "priorities." Remembering the *Challenger* may help you pay close attention to your own priorities about the relevance of information.

Chart a Course: Propose a Conscious Observer's Direction

Mapping the territory with conscious observation provides a sharp focus of awareness. Quantum Leaders then direct their conscious observation to chart a course along a specific path for the more immediate and localized environment.

> *Action Idea: Take to the battlefield.* Go into the trenches when necessary to direct action. Provide others direction when they falter along the path. Abraham Lincoln illustrated this aspect of conscious observation when he practically lived at the War Department during crucial Civil War battles. He slept on a sofa so he could get information as soon as possible. He would peer over the telegrapher's shoulder and react instantly to breaking news. Lincoln took to the battlefield himself when he was dissatisfied with General McClellan's lack of aggressiveness in a battle for Norfolk, Virginia. Consciously observing, Lincoln traveled to a point near Norfolk where the Union troops were bogged down while McClellan stalled farther down the line. The president personally ordered an artillery assault, proceeded down the coast, and then walked ashore to scout the ideal spot for an amphibious landing. When Lincoln returned to the fort, he ordered an attack in which his troops quickly captured the city.

Quantum Perception: The Dual-Angle Lens

Futurist Alvin Toffler once said, "You have to think the big things while doing the small things so the small things go in the right direction." Ideal Quantum Leaders perceive with a combination of vision and conscious observation. They use the long-range, wide-angle lens to perceive the extended path for their organization, and they zoom in to uncover the day-to-day bumps and alternate routes along the way.

Bill Gates of Microsoft displays this dual-action Quantum Leader capability. He is as likely to check for mathematic errors in handouts and overhead slides as he is to critique fuzzy long-term marketing strategies. Ray Kroc, McDonald's Restaurants founder, could see with both the long-term and close-up eye. On Kroc's numerous visits to McDonald's franchises around the world, he checked on every detail, such as how hot the french fries were, while also keeping in mind his overall vision: "Quality, Cleanliness, and Service." Barry Diller supports his vision for QVC by conscious observation. He interrupts what he is doing to watch QVC programming or to attend to the rival Home Shopping Network (HSN). If he notices HSN selling lots of pillows, he might suggest that QVC offer them also.

The capacity to perceive simultaneously with a wide-angle and a zoom lens might appear to require extraordinary perceptual ability. Yet we all have that capacity of consciousness. Think about driving a car. We can perceive both a changing traffic light several hundred yards away and observe the moving needle of the speedometer, less than two feet away. Consider your experience reading this book. While one element of your awareness focuses on the words, you can simultaneously be aware of how to apply an action idea in your office. Consciousness is a quantum phenomenon. It is boundless and fluid information-energy, not hard and inflexible like solid matter.

Action Idea: Practice dual vision. Identify an organization-wide, long-term issue that you believe needs attention. Then specify a detail in your immediate environment that requires concern. Spend 10 minutes each day consciously connecting the big picture issue with the detail. Play with ways to integrate and enfold them into each other. This practice will help you develop the spontaneous ability of the dual-angle-focused Quantum Leader-as-perceiver.

7

Go Into the G.A.P.

"We can only achieve quantum steps of improvement if we get the organization looking at the issues in totally new ways."

—*George Gerhard Schulmeyer, president and CEO of Asel*

What enables the Quantum Leader's consciousness to perceive what others don't and process information from a unique perspective? How does their consciousness operate in distinctive ways? The Quantum Leadership model indicates that leaders interact with the leadership arena by moving their consciousness into "the G.A.P."—the place where they "gain another perspective" of awareness.

Going into the G.A.P. means opening awareness to new ways of observing, interpreting, and evaluating information. From the G.A.P., Quantum Leaders break the boundaries of conditioned perception that restrict attention and limit or negatively affect judgment. Operating from the G.A.P. allows Quantum Leaders to get into a state of "not knowing" so they can then adopt an information-receiving attitude of finding out. When Quantum Leaders go into the G.A.P., they use expanded levels of consciousness so they can step outside an existing paradigm, create an organizational vision, and consciously observe the important interactions that make up day-to-day work activities.

Three Approaches Into the G.A.P.

Quantum Leaders go into the G.A.P. from three approaches. They:

1. Seek information from alternate sources.
2. Expand their interpretative range.
3. Increase their response options.

Seek Information From Alternate Sources

J. W. Marriott, Jr., visits his hotel chain's kitchens, laundry, and telephone reservation centers to find out what is working and if anything is not up to standard. These are not the typical stomping grounds for CEOs of global corporations. Marriott's behavior illustrates the process of seeking information from alternate sources.

Quantum Leaders go into the G.A.P. by seeking information from new, different, untapped, forgotten, previously overlooked, or typically ignored sources. The process compares to expanding from a 30-channel cable TV to a 500- or 5,000-station offering. Quantum Leaders hook their consciousness into the broadest range of information available to get more and different input from more and different sources. This is a conscious, intentional process. Rather than waiting for apples to fall, Quantum Leaders shake the tree.

Opening up the channels of awareness might seem obvious, yet many companies have faltered because they stopped processing or did not fully process the environment's available information-energy. Quantum Leaders distinguish themselves because what should be the commonsense practice of seeking information from alternate sources is not common practice.

Four general mechanics describe how Quantum Leaders go into the G.A.P. and enhance their information seeking:

1. Stop, look, and listen.
2. Audit with the five senses.

3. Attend to new channels.
4. Mine the consciousness in others with question power.

These mechanics do not guarantee finding any particular information. Rather, they are the instruments Quantum Leaders can use to hunt more effectively as they map the territory and chart a course.

Stop, Look, and Listen

Quantum Leaders stop, look, and listen to the information-energy that flows through their organization. They stop their normal routine, look around their operation, and listen to what people are saying. These simple directives become simple actions only after people try them and realize their value. Stop, look, and listen (SLL) turns up information receptivity so people can take in all the signals.

> *Action Idea: Take an SSL pause.* Take a break from your busy schedule each day and get out of your office, away from your normal routine. Then go somewhere different in your organization. Visit the loading dock. Stop by the employee cafeteria. Go into the stock room. Talk to someone you usually do not talk to—maybe the receptionist or the server in the soup line. Pick the brains of a mail clerk. Visit with the company president. Contact your customers directly. Look for information to identify a problem or an opportunity. Listen for a way to resolve the difficulty or exploit the possibility. Take an SSL pause at different times during the day. Vary your SSL routine, but always focus on looking and listening in different places.
>
> *Action Idea: Perform "curiosity calisthenics."* Set aside 10 to 15 minutes perhaps once a month for curiosity calisthenics, an inquiring mind. Nose around, snoop, and explore things that are new or not part of your standard routine. Pretend you are in the attic among a bunch of stuff

that you might recognize but have not looked at lately. Curiosity calisthenics build up attention power to focus the power of the Quantum Leader within.

Action Idea: Work the night shift. Work the night shift (or any other different time slot) to seek insights about activity during different times and to expose yourself to new sources of data.

Action Idea: Reshuffle your calendar. Vary your daily routine. Instead of holding the standard 10:00 A.M. meeting every Tuesday, next week schedule the meeting at a different time or in a new place to bring a new perspective to the meeting. Rather than eating lunch every day at noon, go earlier tomorrow and then a little later the next day.

Action Idea: Conduct a "what's not working" analysis. A "what's not working" analysis identifies problems before they blow up. It directs you to confront obstacles that stifle effectiveness. Be on the lookout for what's not working by stopping, looking, and listening for problems. Then find ways to resolve any problems you uncover.

Action Idea: Review previous action ideas. Many of the action ideas in previous chapters guide you to stop, look and listen—for example, *Fix your sights on nonprescribed areas* (Chapter 2); *Expand your field into different parts of the organization* (Chapter 3); *Adopt a daily opportunity/problem search, Conduct an attention analysis,* and *Perform "AA" for 15 minutes a week* (Chapter 5); and *Watch the message board* (Chapter 6).

Audit With the Five Senses

Quantum Leaders go into the G.A.P. by using their full range of sensory input. They open their perception to new sources of information by auditing with their five senses to feel, hear, see, smell, and even taste what's going on. I once asked an R&D scientist in the Procter & Gamble food division how he knew he had a good cookie, cake mix, or other bakery product. He smiled, then stuck his tongue out at me. I was a little put off by the gesture, but I figured it meant something, so I kept quiet. "I taste it," he then said with a full belly laugh. He explained that if his taste test caused him to spit the food out, the lab kept working on the product. If he chewed it but would not swallow, he talked with the rest of the R&D staff about possible improvements. If he took the food home to his wife and kids and they liked it, he might then talk to the marketing group.

A five-sense audit tunes your attention to sensory data that others no longer recognize or discount. I have consulted with many organizations that have work areas so noisy you have to shout at the person next to you to be heard. I wonder whether anyone else's eardrums ring after being in those noisy work areas. I have sat with managers in hundreds of meetings for thousands of hours on extremely uncomfortable chairs. I wonder if anyone else is in touch with how difficult it is to keep the upper part of the anatomy alert while the lower end becomes numb. I have watched dozens of presenters project blurry images on screens, use tiny typefaces that no one beyond the second row can read, and keep the lights so bright the projected image is washed out. I wonder what these presenters see when they look out at the audience. Quantum Leaders go into the G.A.P. with heightened sensory alertness. They hear, see, touch, smell, and taste a need or potentiality for action.

> *Action Idea: Conduct regular five-sense audits.* Sit in your staff assistant's chair for a while. Look at a computer operator's screen for a few hours. Use a craftsperson's tools for a typical task. Ride in the work vehicles your staff drive. Eat the cafeteria food your company serves. Conduct your regular work activities for a full day in the office space where your employees work. Listen to the noises hammering away in your organization. Use your five senses to experience what is going on in these areas.

Action Idea: Master listening. Listening is a part of a five-senses audit, but I add this action idea as a way to reinforce its importance. For many people, listening means thinking about what *they* are going to say when the speaker stops talking rather than paying full attention to the speaker. This style of listening obviously limits the capacity to perceive possibilities. Effective listeners tune their full awareness on the speaker to understand the message. Such listening is a discipline that requires focus and repeated practice. Take a listening skills course. Model yourself on others whom you feel are good listeners. Do whatever it takes to open your ears, quiet your mind, and shut your mouth so you can hear what others are saying and understand what they mean.

Attend to New Channels

Quantum Leaders go into the G.A.P. when they consciously accept information from new or different channels, that is, intentionally expose themselves to alternate data sources. Part of Japan's rise to economic excellence stems from its unflinching willingness to take in data from new channels. This willingness to go into the G.A.P. originated in 1868 when the Emperor Meiji announced the Five Articles Imperial Oath: "Japan will be receptive to knowledge and technology from whatever source it comes. Japan will send students to the United States and Europe, and will invite foreign experts to come to Japan and disseminate their knowledge to the Japanese." This oath, says Chin-ning Chu in *The Asian Mind Game,* has served as the focus of Japanese economic and political objectives ever since.

Action Idea: Read Literature outside your field/interests. Reading just about any book or periodical outside your field can expand your capacity to perceive from the G.A.P. For example, *Scientific American* addresses discoveries that relate to everyday life. *CD ROM World* describes the latest advances in CD-ROMs, a technology that is certain to become part of the workplace's information processing efforts. I read physics books and magazines to expand my understanding of leadership, management, and organizational development.

Action Idea: Watch different news commentary shows. News shows offer a variety of angles on current information. Most people have their favorite show and ignore the others. Watch a different news show this week to seek an insight or a new perspective on relevant issues.

Action Idea: Read about important figures in history. In reading about Lord Louis Mountbatten many years ago, I learned the importance of building relationships as a foundation in manifesting the leadership field. Mountbatten was assigned as the last viceroy of India when Great Britain agreed to give up colonial rule over the country. He had the difficult task of dividing India among the quarrelsome factions of Hindus, Muslims, and Sikhs. The first time Mountbatten met delegates of each group, he was besieged with demands about their needs, but he skillfully deflected these attacks by claiming that he was completely unprepared to talk business until he "made the proper acquaintance" of the people. This relationship-building action helped him win the favor of each group so that he could work with them effectively. Mountbatten's model is still relevant today. Reading about historical figures, if you do not already attend to this channel, can suggest useful ideas.

Mine the Consciousness Around You With Question Power

Quantum Leaders do not have to be the sole source of information. No matter how much time they spend using stop, look, and listen, five-sense audits, or attending to new channels, they can miss important waves of information, so they rely on others to feed them information that will help them go into the G.A.P.

Quantum Leaders realize that people who are sure they have the answers stop asking questions, and people who stop asking questions rarely venture beyond the prescribed path.

When Dr. Joseph Hoeg was head of the Range Directorate at the Naval Air Warfare Center in Patuxent River, Maryland, he mined the consciousness of others through question power. The Range Directorate employs over 200 people located in ten offices, all over the sprawling naval base. Every Friday, he drove from office to office, visiting various sites and asking questions to help him tune in to alternate sources of information.

Questions excavate ideas, choices, possibilities, solutions, and alternatives, and they drive the software of consciousness to combine and integrate information. They also determine what we pay attention to, so good questions lead to more focused attention power and more refined discrimination so that better answers can be discovered. Quantum Leaders do not have all the answers, but they can ask questions to uncover possible answers.

Quantum Leaders use questions to focus others' awareness toward uncovering problems and finding potential ways to solve them. Brian Dumaine, writing in *Fortune* magazine, explained how Mike Walsh used question power while he was CEO at Union Pacific. He reached into the ranks and asked everyone he could contact, "If you were CEO of this company, what would you do?" Walsh commented, "The people inside your company know a lot more than you think they do."

Quantum Leaders use question power to plug into critical information from all sources: secretaries, customers, suppliers, managers, and line and staff employees. Quantum Leaders view every person as a satellite dish that is connected to some meaningful wavelength of information-energy. These people become idea givers who can fuel the Quantum Leader-as-perceiver's awareness.

Walt Disney mastered the use of questions to gather input from others. Whenever a new project, script, or idea was launched, he would display it on a wall-sized whiteboard. He scrawled the question "How can we improve this?" at the top of the wall as an invitation for everyone's response. People wrote their ideas, suggestions, solutions, and comments all over the wall. Then Disney would review the wall and use the best ideas. He involved the collective consciousness of his entire team to help him get into the G.A.P. and to expand his perceptual capacity.

Any questions can uncover the potentially useful information pulsating within your organization, but eight categories will maximize your ability to go into the G.A.P.: understanding, solution, action, meaning, dumb, possibility, alternative, and necessity questions. The acronym USA MD PAN will help you remember all of them.

> *Action Idea: Ask U—understanding questions.* Understanding questions direct people to clarify the facts or information needed to comprehend a situation, and they focus attention on the details that help make important distinctions—for example, "What do we need to understand about this situation?" "What don't we know about this situation?" "What facts are we missing or misinterpreting?" "What is the difference or similarity between this and that?"

> *Action Idea: Ask S—solution questions.* Solution questions create awareness of specific ways to overcome problems, and they funnel creativity and clarity into potentially workable choices. Use S questions to converge thinking on particular choices to chart a course—for example, "What choices might solve this problem?" "How can we improve the outcome in this case?" "What direction would help us take advantage of this situation?"

> *Action Idea: Ask A—action questions.* Action questions translate thoughts into behavior and clarify the specific steps needed to carry out solutions. Ask action questions to chart a specific course toward a goal—for example, "What

actions do we need to take?" "What specific behaviors do we need to perform?"

Action Idea: Ask M—meaning questions. Meaning questions help people consider what is important and why they should take any action or consider any choices. They get at core values and purposes. Ask meaning questions to clarify intentions and define underlying motivations—for example, "What is important to us?" "Why does this matter to us?" "Why would we want to do this?"

Action Idea: Ask D—dumb questions. Dumb questions invoke the wisdom of the old adage, "The only dumb question is the one you don't ask." After asking a bunch of USA M questions, ask yourself if there are any questions that have not been asked. People usually do not ask questions because they are afraid they will look foolish, or they think they should perhaps already know the answer. Instead, ask every dumb question you can think of, which means *never do not* ask a question. As Aristotle said, "When you ask dumb questions, you get a smart answer."

Action Idea: Ask P—possibility questions. Possibility questions stretch thinking beyond existing boundaries, opening up new vistas. They ask people to imagine what might be or what could be—for example, "If there was a way to do it, what would it be?" "If you could improve this in any way possible, how would you do it?" "What might be a way to solve this problem?"

Possibility questions are especially potent when consciousness stalls or will not move further. For example, use a possibility question the next time you hear someone close the doors of perception. If someone says, "It won't work" or "There's no sense in focusing on that," respond, "Well, if it could work, what would we do?" or "Okay, but if there was a useful way to focus on the issue, how would we do it?" In my experience, asking possibility questions has a powerful impact. People who initially shut down their awareness often pause, then immediately restart their thinking. Consciousness moves with possibility questions.

Action Idea: Ask A—alternatives questions. People usually do not bother thinking of additional answers after they fix on the "right one." Searching for the second, third, and fourth "correct answer" can break boundaries that limit awareness. Ask alternatives questions to accomplish such breakthroughs. These questions are especially important because of the classical physics conditioning that guided most people's schooling. The Newtonian assumption of linear, cause-and-effect reality has led most people to think that problems have one solution and that there is one right answer to each question. Indeed, the hundreds of murderous multiple-choice tests we took in school were written to comply with the one-right-answer logic of the classical physics mind-set. Habituated to this approach, we close up our thinking shop (and we feel good about it!) when we get *the* right answer.

Quantum Leaders shatter such thinking by accepting that other answers could have value. They use what Roger Von Oech, in *A Whack on the Side of the Head,* calls "the second right answer." Ask alternatives questions to accumulate multiple answers—for example, "What else is a correct answer?" "What are *some* answers?" (as opposed to "What is *the* answer?") and "What else would solve the problem?"

Action Idea: Ask N—necessity questions. Necessity questions focus on what must be done to carry out possibilities and alternatives, directing attention to the practical details needed to make things happen. To balance the divergent, no-holds-barred thinking of possibility and alternatives questions, use the convergence provided by necessity questions—for example, "What must we do to accomplish this?" "What specifics must we consider?" and "How must we respond to [a particular issue]?"

Expand Your Interpretative Range

Quantum Leaders gain another perspective when they consciously interpret or evaluate information from a new, different, overlooked, or previously discarded level of awareness. They expand their interpretative range of consciousness to comprehend information from another perspective.

The mind has evaluative filters through which information is recognized, accepted, ignored, or rejected. The brain responds to data by comparing new information with an existing, accepted framework of past experience, a storehouse of impressions or established set of mental models. For example, a production supervisor might evaluate marketing projections for new product orders with the orders from previous years. Or a strategic planning group might evaluate the impact of new technological trends in its industry by comparing them to established technologies and existing trends.

Most people reject, ignore, perceive as meaningless, fail to consider fully, or even denounce and demonize new information when they cannot create a reasonable match with past experience or when the information does not fit their biases. For example, the production supervisor might evaluate the new product order projections as "way out of line" because they do not fit the fairly stable number of orders that marketing has taken over the past several years. The supervisor might even question marketing's motives by thinking, "Marketing is probably trying to impress someone upstairs." Similarly, the strategic planning group might evaluate a new technological trend as unimportant for the industry if it does not fit into the established technology or direction of the existing trend. The strategic planners might even denounce the proposed new trend as "pie in the sky" and something that "will never happen."

When information does not fit with an established mental set, consciousness stalls. People literally do not even consider the information since it is off their existing mental scan. Trapped in the logic of such an evaluative filter, there is little chance to gain another perspective.

To illustrate the process of how evaluative filters work, consider Figure 7-1. How would you interpret the three data points outside the pattern created by the bulk of the data points?

Most people cling to old mental models and do not consider data outside the boundaries. They suggest the three points in Figure 7-1 are outliers caused by measurement error or an indication of some eccentricity. Thus, people say, the three points should be eliminated; they are unimportant because they do not fit the linear line created by the majority of the data points. However, it might be that these three points are the significant first indicators of a new, larger, more important pattern of the data, as suggested in Figure 7-2.

Ignoring information that does not fit an established pattern can spell disaster. In the early 1970s, heads of the American car companies assumed the supply of cheap oil would last for many years. As a result, they discounted the Arab oil cartel as a possible threat to their industry. U.S. auto industry moguls also believed that American car buyers' tastes were standardized and stable. No radical changes in cars were needed, they judged, so

Figure 7-1. The impact of evaluative filters.

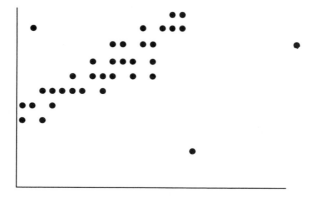

Figure 7-2. New patterns of information.

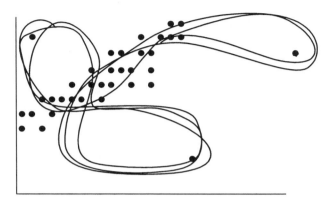

innovations available in Japanese autos would not dent Detroit's market share. Quantum Leaders recognize the hazards of restrictive interpretations and restructure their interpretative range to process information from a more expanded level.

Restructuring requires the full power of intention directed toward the information evaluation process, and it demands the full power of attention focused on the interpretative filters used to accept or reject information. Quantum Leaders consciously focus on establishing a more open and flexible range of interpretation in terms of three factors:

1. Assumptions
2. Beliefs
3. Judgments

Quantum Leaders identify and challenge their assumptions to uncover faulty or inappropriate ways of interpreting information, clarify and identify limiting beliefs that inhibit them, and define and overcome biases that restrict their judgment. These efforts may not always indicate a clear path to success, but they can restructure an awareness to provide the possibility to perceive what others don't.

Assumptions

Assumptions underlie the way we interpret issues. We make assumptions about whether a particular person can perform a task, and we respond accordingly. We assume a certain group will respond to conflict negatively, and we prepare for a battle. A competitor announces a new product, and we make assumptions about how the product will affect our market share.

Some assumptions are obvious to us; that is, we know that our interpretation is based on an assumption, an idea in our mind, as opposed to information. But assumptions can be so deeply embedded in our awareness that we are oblivious to how they guide our thinking and behavior. Quantum Leaders, aware that assumptions are a necessary part of thinking, bring these assumptions to the surface to minimize being guided by faulty assumptions.

> *Action Idea: Identify your assumptions.* Spend time thinking about the assumptions you make when you consider any particular information. To uncover hidden assumptions on a particular issue, think about specific, concrete categories. For example, what assumptions have you made about time, money, equipment, other resources, and the people in your organization? What assumptions do you have about what will work, will not work, or cannot work? What do you take for granted as "true"? What do you discard as "meaningless"? Answers to these questions reveal some of your assumptions. Identify them, and list them on paper. Then define them in terms of an initial set of assumptions, and plot out assumptions that branch off from the initial set. Be self-referred; recognize that these are assumptions you created. Then from this self-referred place, try the next action idea.
>
> *Action Idea: Clarify the relevance of your assumptions.* Answer these questions for assumptions you discover. "What

makes this assumption relevant now?" "What causes me still to consider this a meaningful assumption?" "Why is this assumption no longer valid?" "Do I want to operate with this assumption?" These questions direct your attention to clarify existing assumptions. Refer back to your inner self and ask, "Are these really valid assumptions??" Then take the next action step.

Action Idea: Generate alternate assumptions. Generate a list of alternate assumptions for those you identified. Consider assumptions that contest the ones you created above. Then view the list and ask yourself, "How could the alternate assumptions be true?" "How could both sets of assumptions be valid?" "What new assumptions can be created by combining the assumptions?" Challenge yourself to break through restrictions created by limiting assumptions.

Action Idea: Enroll in "Toyota Tech." "Our current success is the best reason to change things," a statement by Iwao Isomura of Toyota reported in *Fortune* magazine (November 19, 1990), is the motto of "Toyota Tech," the educational division of Toyota Motor Company. Enroll in this school. That is, adopt this way of thinking to direct your consciousness toward the assumption that continuous improvement is essential. Make your course of study ongoing innovation and the deliberate commitment to exploit possibilities.

Beliefs

Beliefs reflect an integrated network of assumptions that guide our interpretation of reality. They provide the ability to succeed, because people with strong beliefs can overcome almost any obstacle. Beliefs also control how we evaluate information. Limiting beliefs virtually imprison our awareness in outdated or useless ways of interpreting information. For example, at one time, no one believed humans could run a four-minute mile. Science even "proved" this by analyzing the human muscle structure and the body's wind resistance. Yet one year after Roger Bannister broke the "impossible" barrier, thirty-seven others did it. Within two years, over 300 people had run as fast. Now numerous high school students crack the four-minute mile every year.

Limiting beliefs become mind-numbing barriers to new frontiers and alternate avenues of interpretation. Reigning scholars of his time scoffed when Copernicus suggested that the sun, not earth, was the center of the solar system. His scientific evidence was dismissed because it ran contrary to the beliefs of the day.

Quantum Leaders embrace the maxim, "What you believe, you achieve." Quantum Leaders go into the G.A.P. to operate from an "all possibilities" belief system. They restructure their awareness and open themselves to believe that solutions and prospects exist.

Cynics often mock those who hold "all possibilities" beliefs. Doubters claim they "know better" than those who adopt the mind-set of a "naive enthusiast." John Wooden, winner of eleven NCAA basketball championships in 12 years of coaching at UCLA, offers another belief in his book, *They Call Me Coach:* "It's what you learn after you know it all that counts."

> *Action Idea: Distinguish your beliefs from information.* Distinguish beliefs from information to avoid faulty beliefs— those not based on the pulse of the most useful, most relevant information to help operate in the leadership arena. Identify your general beliefs or those that relate to a particular leadership arena using the same process described in the *Identify your assumptions* action idea. Then identify the most current, relevant information. Next notice how your beliefs shape your interpretation. Focus on considering how useful, valid, and positive those beliefs are. Using the procedure in the *Generate alternate assumptions* action idea, create a set of new, more effective beliefs by

reshaping your beliefs about the updated information you have generated.

Action Idea: Adopt an "impossible belief" system for a specific time period. Spend a few minutes every so often suspending a belief about what is "impossible." For example, if you believe doubling your market share is impossible, suspend that notion and believe it could happen. With this new belief, how would you behave? Thinking in the "impossible range" helped Texas Instruments dominate the semiconductor industry over giants such as RCA, Sylvania, GE, Westinghouse, Philco-Ford, and Raytheon. George Gilder wrote in his *Microcosm* that Mark Sheppard, a TI manager, explained, "Those companies all knew things that were impossible. We didn't." A few minutes each day in the "impossible range" reengineers your awareness.

Action Idea: Look back 100 years. To open up your belief system, recall that in 1890, there were no space shuttles, no satellite television, and no frozen meals you could prepare in a microwave oven. In 1890, very few people would have believed those technologies were even possible. What beliefs do you hold today that limit your considering possibilities?

Action Idea: Spend time considering how the past cannot be a meaningful guide for the future. Almost any busy person in today's changing, complex, competitive environment knows that the past is not a precise predictor of the future. Certainly the past can provide useful insights, but relying on it in a deterministic way is inappropriate. Yet the classical physics belief in a cause-and-effect world still remains deep within our awareness because it offers stability and security. Tinker with this programmed mental model. Spend some time considering how the past *cannot* be a meaningful guide for the future. Imagine that yesterday, last week, or last year has no impact on the future.

What information comes to your awareness to guide you now? Incorporate this information into the course you chart.

Action Idea: Do some belief busting. Belief busting directs you to explore possibilities that normally are unbelievable. Imagine that your organization has no morale problems, or that all work is done exactly on time and exceeds all expectations. If this "impossible" reality *were* true, what would you do differently?

Action Idea: Develop 100 possibilities. Limiting beliefs can be overcome by exploding boundaries. "Develop 100 possibilities" means generating 100 potential ways (that is what it says: *100*) you could overcome an obstacle or exploit an opportunity. This action idea works best for those who really want to think big. To hit 100, imagine that you have no restraints. Do not let normal reality loom too large while you are developing your list. After you have your 100, propose ways to turn at least some of these possibilities into realities.

Judgments

What ideas are you in love with that cloud your mind? Judgments form cognitive filters and biases that can solidify decision making into rigid and limited categories. Quantum Leader-as-perceivers go into the G.A.P. to restructure their judgment and open it up to alternative rulings.

Action Idea: Learn rather than disagree. The next time you disagree with an idea, adopt a learning posture. Rather than argue for your point of view, say, "What else can you tell me about that?" Consider what inner judgments caused you to disagree immediately. Review these positions to determine how useful they are to you.

Action Idea: Create a judgment list. Over the next week, keep a list of all the judgmental statements or comments you make or think. This thinking may cloak your openness to new, potentially useful information. Consider which of these judgments you might suspend in the future. Establish the intention *not* to use those judgments for a specific time period.

Action Idea: Reverse your position. When you find yourself disagreeing with someone, take that person's position for a while. Pay attention to the judgments that caused you to take your initial position. Consider how those judgments might restrict your perceptual alertness. Focus on eliminating a judgment for a particular time frame.

Action Idea: Be your own devil's advocate. Switch the tables on yourself, and play the devil's advocate with your position, adopting the *opposite* of your point of view to gain an alternate perspective. Overzealous attachment to one judgment limits your ability to recognize new possibilities or alternate approaches to problems.

Action Idea: Find 10 reasons why you are wrong.

Action Idea: Find 10 reasons why the other person is right. Both of these action ideas redirect your awareness to new reference points of judgment. They compel you to get outside the boundaries of your own thinking.

Increase Your Response Options

Once Quantum Leaders perceive a problem or a possibility, they can chart a course for action. The third way Quantum Leaders approach the G.A.P. is to increase their response options to information. They follow Sun Tzu's advice in *The Art of War:* "Don't be bound by established procedures." Quantum Leaders thrive on figuring out how to combine, integrate, and use information in new response modes. With more information and a more open interpretative range, response options will naturally increase. In addition, Quantum Leaders enhance their potential options by going into the G.A.P. and consciously responding with new, untried, or previously abandoned ways to respond.

Quantum Leaders increase their response options when they:

1. Take an experimental approach.
2. Rely on intuition.

Experimentation and intuition may result in success, or they may not. In the quantum reality, no response provides a certain outcome, and no guarantees can be made about what will happen. The purpose of experimentation and intuition is to open streams of consciousness that offer new ways to chart a course of action.

Take an Experimental Approach

Quantum Leaders experiment with choices. They are willing to try an approach, knowing that they cannot predict the outcome. They experiment with various possible paths and with new ways to act. They consider multiple scenarios. Quantum Leaders know that the first step toward mediocrity is a culture of conformity, so they try something new—something they believe in—and if it bombs, they review the experiment to find out what they learned.

Barry Diller, head of the QVC network, described to the *Los Angeles Times* (January 5, 1992) his experiment to create a winner in the global entertainment and communications business:

> Who knows if any of what I'm saying makes sense? That's the most important lesson in this business: That these morning-line prognostications are invariably wrong. Nobody knows what's going to make a good movie. Forget about all the deals and all the theories.

All I know from is, "This is a good idea, and I'm going to pursue it".

Action Idea: Become a "new" Mr. Wizard every day. Do you remember Mr. Wizard, the wily TV scientist who performed incredible science demonstrations? He was actually demonstrating knowledge that previous research had already discovered. Mr. Wizard was teaching us about the past rather than taking us into the unknown. Become a "new" Mr. Wizard by performing an "experiment" in which you find out what will happen by a new response rather than verify old knowledge. Try a new response; then review the experiment as a way to increase your options for the future.

Action Idea: Adopt a learning approach. Every experiment provides data. Adopting a learning approach means making use of those data. Anchor this idea into your awareness: Whatever happens, you will gain useful information when you experiment with a response.

Rely on Intuition

Intuition is the quality of thinking that we cannot explain rationally. Logic is the outcome of the learning process, not the process itself. We think logically about a problem only after we understand it. Understanding, says George Gilder in *Microcosm*, comes from an "elusive process of pattern matching and association," which we label intuition. No reason can describe the flashes of insight and synergistic realizations people sometimes have in response to information. These flashes are quantum leaps of awareness that defy classical physics logic. We label them intuitive because no linear logic describes them. Quantum Leaders learn to trust these experiences when responding from the G.A.P.

Lee Iacocca's intuition drove Chrysler back to the convertible car line. Iacocca had a hunch about the marketability of ragtops, a line all American auto manufacturers had eliminated years before. Deciding to test his feeling, Iacocca directed the production plant to make him a convertible; he was going to experiment. The production chief explained that it would take some time to design the convertible, retool the manufacturing line, and build the prototype. In response, Iacocca clarified the meaning of his directive: He wanted the car *tomorrow*, so "just cut the top off a car and make it look presentable."

The next day Iacocca wheeled his makeshift convertible through the streets of Detroit. When he got back to the office, the decision was clear to him. Based on the positive looks on the faces of those who saw the car, Iacocca "just knew" the car would sell.

Takami Takahashi, founder of Minebea, the world's largest maker of miniature precision ball bearings, used his intuition to guide the development of a new company. Takahashi thought he could apply his manufacturing genius in ball bearings to achieve large-scale manufacturing of DRAM computer chips. Many experts said it could not be done, but Takahashi forged ahead anyway. He launched a new firm, NMB Semiconductor, and built a totally automated production facility. By 1988, his company profitably produced 70 million chips per year. Takahashi's response to his critics, wrote George Gilder in *Microcosm*, is, "Successful people surprise the world by doing things ordinary logical people think are stupid. If I listened to logical people, I would never have succeeded."

Perceiving with intuition means sometimes forgetting what you know and relying on inspiration. Paul MacCready designed the first human-powered aircraft. None of his early efforts worked; all his designs were doomed by "traditional thinking." Then he decided to keep aerodynamic principles in mind but to pretend he had never seen an airplane. His intuitive inspiration came from the way red-tailed hawks fly instead of the way machines fly.

Quantum Leaders use their intuition as a complementary power of perception. They know overdependence on logic or hard sensory data can create intellectual indifference and unresponsiveness. On the other hand, excessive use of intuition can lead to idiosyncratic and arbitrary thinking. Taken together, logic and intuition enable the Quantum Leader to command a wider perceptual response range.

> *Action Idea: Follow a hunch.* Follow the next hunch you have about how to respond. Hunches, feelings, inklings, and premonitions are intuitive signals. By following a hunch, you can gauge your intuitive skill. My experience is that the more you use intuition, the better it gets.

> *Action Idea: Contact your intuition.* Intuition lies within the deeper layers of consciousness. Contact your intuition by sitting quietly with your eyes closed and letting your awareness simply be quiet. Pay attention to the signals you get from that settled place of awareness; then consider how to respond to a situation. When you open your eyes, reconsider what your quiet consciousness revealed in the light of practical reality.

Picking Your Spots

You don't have to go into the G.A.P. twenty-four hours a day. Nor do you have to ask questions in a nonstop, machine-gun fashion of everyone you meet. It is not essential that you continually restructure your interpretative range or ceaselessly try new response options.

Quantum Leaders pick their spots by going into the G.A.P. for selected periods each day or week. I recommend people try just one or two of the action ideas in this chapter and go into the G.A.P. for just a few minutes each day. I do not know what you will find, or even if you will find anything that requires leadership initiative. But I do know that if you do not try to perceive anything, you will not find anything. The starting gun for the leadership process will not sound without someone's initiating an interaction with the leadership arena. I imagine that organizations would change very quickly if everyone would spend just 15 minutes every day actively going into the G.A.P.

8

Gain Commitment Through Enlightened Action

"You have to be able, frankly, to sell yourself and the logic of your approach to all those constituencies. You become the human bridge to absolutely everybody."

—*Mike Walsh, former CEO of Tenneco*

Dudley Hanson opened the envelope and noticed the word *rejected* stamped on the cover of his budget proposal. None of the division chiefs and none of his staff colleagues had supported his request. Hanson was chief of the Planning Division of the Army Corps of Engineers in Rock Island, Illinois. The corps was responsible for the navigation facilities of the upper Mississippi River inland waterway system. Significant bulk commodities pass through the system, including agricultural products en route to users in the eastern United States.

In 1986, Hanson had recognized that the system was deteriorating from lack of adequate repair, and without attention it might fail to meet increasing carrying-capacity demands. The waterway system compared to a two-lane road in an age of multilane expressways. When Congress passed the Water Resources Development Act that year, Hanson perceived the congressional appropriation as a key opportunity and decided to request funds for an investigation on how best to make capital improvements to improve the navigational system, so he submitted his budget proposal request in 1987 for the fiscal year 1989 budget. The proposal outlined a request to fund a Planning Division study that would investigate future capital improvement projects. He believed that everyone involved would perceive the budget proposal in the same light he did and assumed the request would be accepted because of the importance of upgrading the facilities.

After the stunning rejection, Hanson tried to sort out what happened. He had clearly perceived that many factors complicated any proposal regarding waterway improvements in this area of the Mississippi. The area is an environmentally sensitive region, recognized by federal law as both a significant national ecosystem and a commercial navigational system. The costs of capital improvements could exceed hundreds of millions of dollars. Moreover, the upper Mississippi is managed by an array of federal, state, and local governmental agencies and advised by a number of pro bono public groups. Any proposal for improvement would have to meet multiple, competing demands from a variety of sources.

But Hanson thought his proposal had taken these complex issues into account, so he decided to go into the G.A.P. to analyze his assumptions and beliefs and perhaps understand how others had interpreted the proposal. The analysis suggested several reasons for the rejection.

As chief of planning, Hanson naturally assumed that funding a planning proposal should be the first step. Hanson also assumed that all of the other division chiefs and senior staff in the Rock Island would recognize and support this approach. Hanson found out that although the chiefs and the staff believed as he did that the navigational facilities needed to be upgraded, they interpreted Hanson's budget request as primarily an attempt to support his own Planning Division. Hanson knew his intentions were not self-serving, but he quickly understood why the other division chiefs and senior staff members did not support the budget. From their frames of reference, they believed the allocation would not serve interests they valued.

Hanson also uncovered the lack of support from his staff colleagues. The Rock Island District played an important role in maintaining and upgrading the national assets the waterway system represented, and everyone associated with the operation was vital to it. Yet he realized that his exhortations to his staff to support the budget request communicated a different message. He had tried to influence them by explaining that, without the funds, the Rock Island District would become a "mere operation and maintenance, custodial organization." Hanson saw how this message violated their values. The operation and maintenance divisions were very capable and vitally important. Hanson had framed his points in a way that alienated the bureaucratically powerful operation and maintenance personnel.

A few months after the budget rejection, Hanson was still intent on improving the navigation facilities of the upper Mississippi River inland waterway system. Armed with the increased discrimination he gained from the analysis of the previous request, he initiated a revised budget for 1990. The request was approved. As of June 1992, studies were underway to ensure the full viability of the navigational systems in the twenty-first century.

Enlightened Action

Dudley Hanson's story shows that it is not enough to map the territory and chart a course to perceive what others don't. To be a leader requires getting others to follow your course (*the first natural law of leadership*). The Quantum Leadership model indicates that the Quantum Leader–follower interaction involves gaining follower commitment by performing enlightened action (Figure 8-1).

The Light Switch

Performing enlightened action resembles turning on a light in a pitch-black room. Few people will move very quickly, if at all,

Figure 8-1. The Quantum Leadership model: Gaining commitment and performing enlightened action.

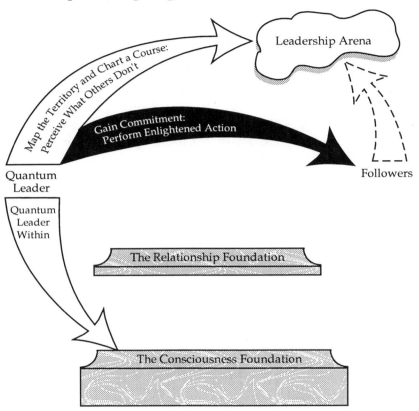

into a dark, unfamiliar room. Yet even a brief flicker of light provides enough awareness to enable them to move ahead. The leadership arena is a risk-filled, uncertain territory. Performing enlightened action dispels the darkness of uncertainty so followers can see the value and have a clear perspective, which motivates them to commit to the leader's direction.

Quantum Leaders enlighten followers with a variety of actions. Inspirational words, such as Martin Luther King's "I Have a Dream" speech, can inspire commitment. Metaphors can illuminate the followers to accept the leader's direction. Mary Kay Ash, founder of Mary Kay Cosmetics, uses the bumblebee as a metaphor to inspire the women who join her organization that they can realize their full potential. Because the bee's body is too heavy for its wings, it should not be able to fly; however, since the bee does not know this, it flies anyway.

Leading by doing can motivate followers. During a raging forest fire in Utah in 1978, Martha Hahn of the Bureau of Land Management (BLM) gained committed followers without saying a word. To contain the huge blaze, which had scorched over 4,000 acres, the BLM needed help from any source. Hahn was given a crew made up of convicts. Her job was to guide these men to contain spot fires, small blazes that jump over an established fire line. When Hahn and the convicts met, they eyed her with suspicion, but she had no time to respond to this signal; they had to contain a spot fire about a mile away. Hahn and her crew raced by truck to the fire, and Hahn quickly gave directions to cut down some burned trees to create a line of demarcation between the burned and the green areas. As the men stood silently, gaping at her, Hahn grabbed an axe and started chopping down a tree. The men watched her in amazement for a few minutes but then joined her. Later, one of the men explained to her, "We aren't used to seeing a girl cut down a tree. Her model inspired them to begin working.

Symbols can also turn on the light to guide followers. A production plant quality team facilitator placed a display at the door of the plant that showed the organization's primary competitor's most successful products. The display served as a symbolic reminder of the quality level the company's products had to achieve to win in the marketplace.

Ray Kroc wanted his McDonalds' shift managers to spend more time at the counter interacting with customers. Kroc felt his vision, "Quality, Cleanliness, Service," could not be achieved without face-to-face customer contact. To get his message across, Kroc had the backs of the office chairs sawed off. He felt the shift managers might not spend so much time in the office if the chairs were uncomfortable.

Dudley Hanson's second budget was approved because he took action that enlightened others. The request enlarged his argument for funding to include the full range of responsibilities that the Rock Island District had. He made a case for ongoing attention to upgrading the navigational infrastructure by improvements in operations and maintenance, major rehabilitation and repair, and capital improvements. Hanson gave recognition to all members of the organization and to their professional duty as stewards of a portion of the operation. His arguments appealed to the strong sense of service in the corps. His new approach also recognized and acknowledged their professionalism. He expanded his frame of reference beyond its impact on the Planning Division to eliminate any perception of parochialism. And he established the important role each group had to play in shaping the future of the corps. For these key followers, Hanson's revised approach had new meaning that attracted them to support him.

The Communication of Meaning

Quantum Leaders use words, metaphors, behavior, and symbols to enlighten followers; however, these methods represent only the surface level of interaction. The real impact of performing enlightened action occurs at the level of the meaning of these methods. Enlightened action is the communication of meaning. Figure 8-2 demonstrates the role of meaning in the communication process. Communication involves the Quantum Leader's idea translated into a message (how the leader maps the territory and the leader's chart for the course), which is transmitted by the leader's words and behaviors, or symbols. The follower receives the message and translates it into the follower's idea of the leader's direction. Quantum Leaders gain committed followers when the meaning as interpreted by the follower is the same as the desired meaning underlying the leaders' idea.

Figure 8-2. The communication process.

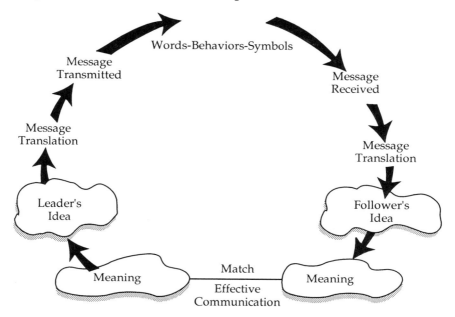

If people get the wrong meaning, they will not follow, or they may go in the wrong direction. When a young FBI agent was put in charge of the supply department, he decided to cut costs by reducing the size of memo paper. FBI Director J. Edgar Hoover received one of the smaller memo sheets and disliked it, so he wrote on the narrow margin, "Watch the borders." For the next six weeks, FBI agents increased surveillance along the Mexican and Canadian borders.

The substance of the communication—what is actually said or done to transmit the message—has impact only in terms of its meaning to the followers. If a message is confusing, the meaning transmitted can negate a leader's impact. Followers interpret some meaning from any message they receive, and the meaning defines the reaction to the leader. Consider the reaction created by Dan Quayle's infamous rewording of the United Negro College Fund's slogan, "A mind is a terrible thing to waste": "What a waste it is to lose one's mind, or not to have a mind, how true that is."

The Quantum Connection

When Quantum Leaders perform enlightened action, a connection of meaning occurs between the leader and the followers. Meaning is structured in consciousness. It is subjective and based in the mind, not objective or defined by matter. Each person's unique, self-referral information processing procedure creates meaning for him or her. For example, downsizing efforts that result in an improved balance sheet are interpreted favorably by stock holders; in contrast, that downsizing means lost jobs and unemployment to company employees.

The classical physics paradigm, which assumes an objective reality, biases our thinking to believe we can communicate a "factually" correct message. For example, George Bush's assertions during the 1992 presidential campaign that the United States was not in an economic recession were technically correct. Based on the traditional economic explanation of number of consecutive quarters of economic growth, the United States had broken out of the recession months before the November 1992 election. Similarly, in 1994, Bill Clinton made justifiable declarations about having accomplished many of his stated campaign objectives. The budget deficit was down, and the crime bill and the North American Free Trade Agreement had been passed.

However, leaders gain followers based on the meaning followers assign to facts, not the facts themselves. Quantum Leadership fields do not exist unless the leader's intended meaning resonates with the followers on their level of self-referral consciousness *(the ninth natural law of leadership)*. The word *communication* shares the same root word with *community, commune, and commonality*. Enlightened action communicates the leader's meaning so that followers understand, accept, and identify with it. The basis of Quantum Leader power, influence beyond authority *(the fourth natural law of leadership)*, lies in a quantum connection—the unity created when the follower's consciousness is enlightened by the meaning of the leader's direction.

Despite the objective "correctness" of their messages, George Bush failed to gain reelection in 1992, and the voters demonstrated what many analysts believed was a sign of rampant dissatisfaction with Bill Clinton in 1994 when they voted a Republican majority into both houses of Congress.

The quantum connection creates rapport, the sense of trust and comfort followers feel towards the leader because they perceive the leader to be like them. Followers commit when they can "relate to," "identify with," and "have confidence" in the leader and when they believe the leader's ideas "make sense" to them. Quantum Leadership explains that the meaning of the message is known in the response the leader gets.

Quantum Leaders increase the probability of getting the response of willing followers by communication flexibility: They use a variety of communication channels to transfer meaning. Quantum Leaders also gain commitment as congruent communicators, which means they speak and behave in ways that mutually reinforce and correspond to the meaning they want to get across. Mixed messages create confused meanings. Communication flexibility and communication congruence transmit the Quantum Leader's message more accurately.

Communication Flexibility

Quantum Leaders are flexible communicators. They rely on a variety of communication channels to get the meaning of their message across.

> *Action Idea: Use symbols to illustrate your direction.* Symbols, such as the competitor's product display placed at the plant door by the quality team facilitator, offer a powerful channel to get across the meaning of your message because they capture the full range of meaning in a kernel of

action. Use symbols to capture the meaning of your direction.

Action Idea: Create a theme event. We have many traditional theme events in America, from Thanksgiving to Flag Day, that create specific meanings. Create a theme event—an empowerment day or a customer satisfaction week—to reinforce your leadership direction. Establish a slogan for it, and then create trappings—pictures, decorations, music, or food—to get the message across to your employees. Make it a memorable event to transmit the meaning of your course of action.

Action Idea: Collect and use stories or metaphors. Everyone loves a good story, and a well-crafted metaphor can create an image that depicts the idea behind your leadership direction. A manager in a large retail operation loves to tell the story about opening a new store on a Saturday, and how the local banker did not believe the manager really needed fifty specially locked cash bags to store the funds collected over the weekend. The store, she said, would never do that much business, so she gave him only twenty pouches. On Monday, the manager dumped the twenty full cash bags on the banker's desk, along with forty plastic trash bags bulging with money. The manager uses the story to illustrate the need to think big.

Action Idea: Put an artifact into your office. A personal artifact placed on your desk or office wall can communicate a powerful message. Louis Katopodis, president of Fiesta Mart, the Houston-based grocer, has a baseball bat leaning in the corner of his office. Katopodis believes people need to "step up to the plate" to meet the challenges of the fast-moving grocery business.

Action Idea: Develop a stump speech. Politicians develop a stump speech that they repeat over and over to get across their key ideas as they race along the campaign trail. Your stump speech should contain the two or three core ideas you want to communicate about your leadership direction. By delivering your speech often enough to reinforce its meaning but not so often it becomes boring, you will put your message across effectively.

The line between reinforcement and boring is, of course, part of the art that you have to continually address when you implement any of these action ideas. The ideas are choices that must always be considered in the larger context, and their use requires your conscious attention and discrimination.

Action Idea: Write for your readers. Written communication is an important source of message transfer. Writing for your readers means considering how they will interpret the words you place on the page, not what you think the words mean. Consider how much time they have to read; then think about whether the writing should be in bullet form, paragraphs, a table, or single sentences. Ask yourself, "When they get this document, how will they make meaning of the direction I am suggesting, based on the words I have written?" A few minutes of reflection will sharpen your written communication.

Communication Congruence

Quantum Leaders communicate with congruence—in other words, what they say and how they say it transmit a consistent message. Communication research, reported by Albert Mehrabian in *Silent Messages*, shows that only 7 percent of a message's meaning is transmitted by words. Thirty-eight percent of meaning is transmitted by tone of voice and 55 percent by nonverbal behavior or body language. During one of the 1994 presidential debates among George Bush, Bill Clinton, and Ross Perot, analysts counted the number of times each candidate blinked while speaking. The number of blinks is said to reveal the speaker's tension level created by a lack of certainty or conviction about the words being spoken. While responding to certain questions, each of the candidates' eyes fluttered often, which implied that their statements meant something other than what the candidate's words implied. Quantum Leaders transmit their meaning more effectively when the words, tone, and body language are congruent.

Action Idea: Listen to a radio talk show. Radio talk show hosts have mastered the art of communicating meaning through sound. They know how to alter their tone of voice and cadence of speech to reinforce the meaning behind their words. Listen to them speak, and model your own speech on those radio talk show hosts you admire.

Action Idea: Vary your speech pattern. Most people can listen much faster than most people talk. Speed up your speech to keep attention. When you want to emphasize a particular point, slow down your speech. Varying your speech pattern keeps followers tuned in and gives you a chance to help your listeners better understand the meaning of your leadership direction.

Action Idea: Take a presentation skills course within the next three months. Most people are not very good at public speaking, and no one can ever be too good at it. You may have to communicate your leadership direction to others in a stand-up presentation. A course on presentation skills can transform your capacity to get across meaning in a congruent and cogent fashion.

Action Idea: Join Toastmasters. Toastmasters is an organization that has mastered the art of developing people's ability to speak in front of groups.

Action Idea: Move your head and body more when you give a presentation. Many people present information in a wooden fashion, using very little body movement. Moving your head and body to emphasize your points increases your communication congruence.

Action Idea: Take an acting lesson in the next two months. Actors know how to speak, behave, and emote in a fashion that convinces us they are the character. An acting lesson will improve your ability to be a more convincing communicator of the meaning of your message.

Action Idea: Watch one live theater performance this month. Model what you see on the stage. Notice how the actors use their full range of voice, body action, and the stage space to get their ideas across. Observe, practice, and then try some of the skills you witness on stage the next time you want to communicate your message.

Action Idea: Watch a TV comedian perform for 10 minutes with the sound turned off. Some TV comedians do not say things that are funny, but many of them know how to use their nonverbal behaviors to reinforce their message congruently. Watch them with the sound off to notice how they communicate nonverbally.

Action Idea: Watch kids at play to notice their body language. Children are almost totally uninhibited in their body motion. They jump, shake, wiggle, and contort themselves in concert with how they feel. By watching them play, you might notice a nuance of behavior you could adopt that would be appropriate to communicate more effectively.

Action Idea: Analyze five TV commercials on video in the next month. Television commercials are brilliantly crafted morsels of meaning. In 15 seconds, the advertisers can say everything they want you to know to motivate you to purchase the product. Analyze TV commercials on video so you can watch them in fast and slow motion to discern how they get a powerful, congruent message across in a few moments.

Action Idea: Study five magazine advertisements a week. Analyze printed advertisements with the same intention as TV ads.

Action Idea: Consciously relax your facial muscles three times a day. When your face tightens, your message is much less positive than when your facial muscles are relaxed. Many people do not realize that they walk around with a stone-faced, impassive look on their face, or that their forehead is furrowed, or their mouth pulled down in a frown. By relaxing your facial muscles, you let go of this unconscious reaction, communicate a more positive picture, and actually use less energy. It takes a lot of exertion to contort our faces into some of the hard looks we hold.

Action Idea: Double your smile rate. People who consistently smile are often thought to have positive attitudes. Doubling your smile rate communicates greater certainty about your ideas. Smiling can mean greater confidence to followers.

Matching Meaning

Enlightened action matches the way followers create meaning. Matching is the Quantum Leader's ultimate power tool to influence others beyond authority. You can create shared meaning by meeting your followers at their level of consciousness and then leading them to your own level of consciousness.

9

Create Shared Meaning

"If you cry 'Forward,' you must make clear the direction you want to go. Don't you see that if you fail to do that and simply call out the word to a monk and a revolutionary, they will go precisely in the opposite directions."

—Anton Chekhov, Russian playwright

While consulting with a large manufacturing company, I attended a meeting with a group of eight managers who were essentially peers. The company had gone through an extensive downsizing, and one of the group's managers, Joel, had been charged with developing a new approach for a work restructuring process. Joel presented his plan to the group, a brief question-and-answer period ensued, and the meeting was then adjourned. The managers would discuss the plan with their staffs and then reconvene the next day for further discussion.

I noticed that one manager, Liz, very obviously favored Joel's plan while another, Robert, was clearly against it, and I asked each in private to explain their positions. Liz thought that Joel's plan was "the right thing for employees whose morale was most important now," and that "Joel's point of view minimized the trauma of what was a tough situation." In contrast, Robert believed that the plan was "a bad approach at this time because it hurt the organization's chances to improve efficiency," and that "Joel's frame of reference was too narrow given the radical changes that had occurred." When I probed the reasons behind their comments, Liz and Robert referred to the same facts and statistics Joel presented to support their completely different interpretations. This difference arose because Liz and Robert processed information differently.

Values and Frames: Sources of Meaning

Quantum Leaders cannot directly control the follower's information processing methods since these methods occur within the follower's consciousness, and therefore they cannot dictate the meaning a follower attributes to the message. However, Quantum Leaders can consciously match the way a follower processes information to influence the meaning that the follower interprets.

Followers create meaning in terms of their values and through the frame of reference they use. *Values* serve as a filter people use to assign meaning about what is good or bad, right or wrong. *Frames of reference* act as windows through which the meaning of information is filtered and as lenses that bring the meaning of information into focus. Joel influenced Liz to follow because his presentation matched her values and frame. Joel failed to gain Robert's commitment because his presentation did not match Robert in these two critical areas.

Quantum Leaders create shared meaning by performing action that matches the follower's values. They can also reframe their initiatives to match or create a frame that a follower can identify with as useful. The better the match of values and frame of reference is, the more effective the transfer of meaning and the greater likelihood the followers will support the leader. Quantum Leaders meet followers at their level of consciousness and then lead followers to the leader's level.

The mechanics of performing enlightened action involve Quantum Leaders' tuning their attention to understand how others create meaning and then adapting to match the follower's process. At times, the leader only has to find the critical 1 percent match to achieve a 100 percent endorsement for the leader's direction. Matching values and reframing are the Quantum Leader's power tools to forge that connection and thereby create shared meaning.

Matching Values

The Values Filter

Values define what people believe is important; they establish what people regard as good or bad, worthy or unworthy, right or wrong. Liz valued employee morale; Robert valued organizational efficiency. People use values as touchstones to measure if they are on or off course and as guides to behavior. Values lie in the deep fabric of consciousness as an executive level of judgment. People process information through their core values, and those values affect the creation of meaning. Values serve as a filter through which we translate information and evaluate its content. People doubt those who do not support their values and become suspicious of those with different values.

Followers identify with the Quantum Leader's message when it is personally significant to them and taps into their core values. When President Kennedy visited Berlin in 1963, he astutely matched the values of the democratic population held hostage within the divided city of the communist-controlled portion of Germany with these words:

> There are many people in the world who really don't understand, or say they don't, what is the great issue between the free world and the Communist world. Let them come to Berlin. There are some who say that Communism is the wave of the future. Let them come to Berlin. . . . And there are even a few who say that it is true that Communism is an evil system, but it permits us to make economic progress, "Lass sie nach Ber-

lin kommen," let them come to Berlin. Freedom has many difficulties and democracy is not perfect, but we have never had to put a wall up to keep our people in to prevent them from leaving us.

The crowds went wild, shouting and cheering their enthusiastic acceptance of Kennedy because his refrain, "Let them come to Berlin," resonated with their values.

Resonating With the Follower's Values

Quantum Leaders identify the followers' values and then reinforce those values with their message. When Jim Renier became vice chairman of Honeywell in 1985, he encountered a company with falling productivity and low morale. He recognized that the values employees felt were most important—truth, trust, and respect—were absent from the workplace. Indeed, he perceived that his organization suffered from a malady that had spread across the United States: an increasing narcissism, with everyone caring only for themselves at the expense of others. So Renier promoted the theme "Respect for People" to indicate his disdain for the "paddle-your-own-canoe" values dominating the workplace. Honeywell employees identified with this message, say Noel Tichy and Mary Anne Devanna in *The Transformational Leader*, and they supported Renier's direction.

Successful political candidates match voters' values by personifying the public's concerns and passions. Bill Clinton's 1992 campaign theme, focused on the domestic economy, illustrates the attraction power behind expressing a value that resonates with the public. In 1940, Winston Churchill gained the prime minister post by tapping into the value held by the British people that they could win the war against Hitler.

Identifying Values

Quantum Leaders identify followers' values by discussing them and by helping people clarify and prioritize values. They carefully listen and observe others, seeking clues to their values, and they clarify their own values as well.

You can create shared meaning with followers when you have a clearly defined set of your own values. You will know which values you share with others that can be used to draw them to you. You will also recognize those whom you will not gain as followers because of serious values conflicts. Recall *the seventh natural law of leadership:* Not everyone will follow. When you cannot match another person's values, that is a signal to move on and try to attract other followers.

> *Action Idea: Clarify your core values.* Spend time determining your core values—those that are ends in themselves. Probe what matters to you by asking, "What parameters do I use to guide my decisions, my thinking, and my approach to life? What is most important to me?" List these values on paper. Then clarify the more primary values behind those on your list by considering, "What does this value provide me?" For example, you might value professional respect, because it provides you with a sense of self-confidence, which you desire as an end in itself. Self-confidence would represent a core value.
>
> After you develop an initial list of values, self-refer, that is, turn within your consciousness to the source of your intention, and prioritize your values. Which values are most essential to you? And are these the values that you really *want* to guide you? By consciously self-referring to your values, your discrimination can choose the values you want. Revise and refine your core values to select a set of your highest-priority values—those that are most essential. Review this refined list on a regular basis, perhaps once a month, to reinforce it and/or update it with further clarification.
>
> *Action Idea: Hold values clarification sessions.* Set aside time to discuss values with others. Use "meaning questions" from the USA MD PAN technique described in

Chapter 7. Ask people to explain what is important to them at work. Discuss which values they rely on to interpret events. Propose a list of values for discussion (e.g., teamwork, expertise, concern for others, honesty, participation) to find out which values they find most compelling. A group of people may have a variety of different values. By clarifying their values, you gain the possibility of finding ways to match those that are important to each person. Furthermore, the values clarification session gives you a chance to define your core values to others, which helps set the tone to guide the discussion toward primary values. That is, following the first action idea in this chapter, your values have been refined to a list of primary values—those that are ends in themselves. Use the same procedure outlined in the first action idea in this chapter to clarify followers' primary values.

Action Idea: Listen for the values messages. Because values are subtle, they can be difficult to uncover; you must consciously listen for them. The statement, "I don't care how long it takes, I just want to get it done," suggests the speaker values good follow-through or results. The statement, "I hope the layoffs are over because I can't go through much more of this," suggests the speaker values stability. "What are the numbers? What's the bottom line here?" suggest the person values precision, accuracy, and accountability. "We need to pull together" suggests the speaker values teamwork and cooperation.

When you think you have identified the values behind the words, clarify the accuracy of your perception by stating it to the speaker. For example, after the statement "I don't care how long it takes, I just want to get it done," restate to clarify by saying, "It sounds as if follow-through is important to you." The person's response will verify if you have discerned the value.

Action Idea: Probe to clarify deeper values. Clarify values by probing the deeper meaning behind each one. Consider a person who says she values money. You can probe this value by asking, "What is important to you about money?" Suppose the person responds, "The ability to take care of my needs." A further probe might be, "What is important about taking care of your needs?" The person might respond, "A sense of security," which would be the deeper, more primary value. The probing process can dig into deeper layers to help clarify core values fully.

Action Idea: Prioritize values through pairing. All values do not hold equal weight. Achievement might be of paramount importance at work, but love and respect might be more important at home. Understand followers' values by asking them to prioritize values in pairs. For example, ask followers, "In this situation, which is more important to you: respect or challenge?" Making such distinctions helps you identify the highest-priority values.

Action Idea: Identify the behavior-value connection. Once you have identified a person's important values, explore the behaviors he or she believes reflect those values. Defining the behavior-value connection is important because values are invisible filters but behaviors are observable. For example, if a person values respect, ask the person to define the specific behaviors that demonstrate respect. If he or she indicates respect is demonstrated by asking people for their opinions, you have a way to match that core value.

Create Shared Meaning by Matching Values

To create shared meaning, communicate your direction (the course you have charted) by matching the values of others. One of the senior partners in a medium-size law firm wanted to expand the business, which meant hiring more lawyers with different specialties. Some of the lawyers resisted this idea because they perceived growth in the number of personnel as a threat to their autonomy (a core value). They worried that a larger organization would be more rigid and structured. The senior partner discovered that job security was their higher-priority value. In the extremely competitive legal services business, a glut of lawyers made it difficult to find a good position, such as the one this law firm provided. The senior partner influenced his colleagues to follow his lead by focusing his message on the increased job security to be gained by expanding the business. More lawyers meant the firm could provide more expertise, positioning it to have more marketing flexibility and the ability to develop a larger client base, which would ensure greater job security for everyone.

> *Action Idea: Translate your direction to match follower values.* Translate your course of action into a message that reinforces values. For example, if people value expertise, communicate your direction by demonstrating your expertise: "I know this direction will pay off because . . . [demonstrate your expertise]." You could also communicate your direction to reinforce how it affects their expertise: "We will learn more about . . . if we do . . ."

> *Action Idea: Communicate values with congruence.* Practice aligning what you say and how you say it to be congruent with the values you are trying to match. For example, to communicate the value of honesty, use a sincere tone and expression. To communicate the value of openness, make eye contact and get out from behind your desk so you do not have a barrier between you and the follower. To communicate the value of challenging experience, speak with enthusiasm. These action ideas sound like common sense, but congruent communication takes practice. Refer to the action ideas in Chapter 8 regarding congruent communication as a guide to improve your skills in this area.

> *Action Idea: Perform action that demonstrates followers' behavior-value connection.* Specific behaviors are indica-

tors of values. You create shared meaning when you use the behaviors that followers have revealed as expressions of their core values.

Action Idea: Say it again, Sam. "Everyone wants to do a good job; everyone wants to make a contribution." Ron Opitz, a manager at Public Service Organization of Oklahoma, a utility company in Tulsa, made this statement to me at least one hundred times during a six-month consulting projecting I conducted with his company. He was expressing one of his core values, which was important to the group he wanted to influence. Opitz's example reveals how to create shared meaning by frequent repetition of key values. Repeat your message to transmit core values. Let people know you really believe in specific values by reminding them again and again of the value's importance.

Reframing

Leon Moore exudes energy and enthusiasm. In May 1991, I asked Moore, the regional commissioner for the Internal Revenue Service's Central Region, how he felt the IRS was doing. "Well," he replied, "we need a $7 billion capital investment for our modernization efforts!" His comment startled me, not only because of what he said but also by the way he said it. Moore seemed almost upbeat. Intrigued, I asked him to explain. Moore replied that when consumers have problems with their bank, they can telephone the institution and almost immediately get a response regarding the cause of the problem. But when taxpayers have problems with their returns, they cannot get such a speedy reply. "We haven't had the computer hardware and software in place to help explain the situation to the taxpayer. Now we know what we need. It will cost us $7 billion to become fully computerized." This did not sound like a very good situation to me, so I said nothing. Then Moore completely changed my perspective when he said, "What an exciting time to work for the IRS!"

Frames and Reframes

Leon Moore illustrated how Quantum Leaders create shared meaning by *reframing:* creating an attractive and positive perspective by putting information into a different context. A mental frame defines the perspective through which we perceive the world. The frame clarifies the picture like a lens that brings an image into focus. We process information and create meaning based on the frame we use. Moore painted a picture of the IRS as experiencing an exciting and challenging period of change. He focused on the IRS's expansion of capacity and ability to serve the public. He could have lamented the problems associated with the use of unsophisticated technology, but he chose a frame that highlighted the positive aspects of the IRS transformation. Moore's action with me was not an isolated incident. In speaking with those who work for him, I discovered that Leon Moore lives the image he presented to me. He consistently views the IRS as an exciting, challenging place to work.

By relabeling and redefining events, reframing allows people to think about things differently, to see another point of view, and to take different factors into consideration. When the frame changes, meaning changes. Quantum Leaders create shared meaning by reframing events so that followers connect with the leader's direction, understanding it as useful, worthwhile, and attractive to follow.

Quantum Leaders recognize that their course of action must be presented in ways that attract willing followers. They know they can create meaning through reframing because there are multiple ways to perceive any experience or situation, and they select a frame that is useful to them and their followers. Katherine Graham, publisher of the *Washington Post*, clarified the subjective reality of a mental frame when she noted that "a mistake is simply another way of doing things."

When people initially share a similar frame of reference

with the leader, it is easier to perform action that enlightens them to follow. In such cases, the leader only has to reinforce the existing, similar frame to establish shared meaning. For example, I have met several other managers at the IRS who share Leon Moore's enthusiasm regarding the organization's status. They do not perceive his comment as a reframe. Instead, they heartily agree that it is an exciting time to work for the IRS.

Quantum Leaders reframe situations when they need to change the focus of attention. Reframing creates shared meaning for those whose prevailing view limits their willingness to follow. Reframing elicits a positive response that unites the leader and follower.

On April 4, 1968, black Americans smoldered with justifiable anger about Martin Luther King Jr.'s murder. Fear of a violent backlash spread across the country because a white man had gunned King down. Bobby Kennedy, on the campaign trail for the presidency, was scheduled to speak in a black neighborhood in Indianapolis. He was the first to bring the news of King's assassination to this crowd. In an effort to soothe those deeply hurt supporters of the inspirational King, Kennedy effectively reframed the tragedy to calm the crowd:

> For those of you who are Black and are tempted to be filled with hatred and distrust at the injustice of such an act, against all white people, I can only say that I feel in my own heart the same kind of feeling. I had a member of my family killed, but he was killed by a white man. But we have to make an effort in the United States, we have to make an effort to understand, to go beyond these rather difficult times.

Effective reframes result in comments from followers such as, "Well, when you look at it that way, I do agree" or "Yes, from that perspective, I do feel okay about taking this course of action."

Reframing requires stepping out of trained patterns of perception to change the meaning of events. Perceptual processes can become trapped in routinized models or maps, which limit our capacity to perceive information. Quantum Leaders direct their consciousness to break through their bounded cognitive patterns by mapping the territory and charting a course to perceive what others don't, and by going into the G.A.P. Then Quantum Leaders perform enlightened action by reframing situations so that others also drop limiting models and accept the leader's direction. Quantum Leaders reframe to redraw the follower's mental maps.

Understanding the Follower's Existing Frame

Reframing begins by identifying the follower's existing frame. Quantum Leaders seek to understand the context or backdrop that establishes the follower's existing perspective by asking questions, such as, "What does that mean to you?" For example, José, a supervisor in a service company, recently told me that Bobbie, a new manager, "doesn't support our real mission." I asked José, "What do you mean, 'doesn't support?'" He responded, "Bobbie is more interested in costs than customers." I sought further understanding of the frame by asking, "What do you mean she is 'more interested in costs than customers?'" José clarified his frame by telling me, "Bobbie has held dozens of meetings with the finance people, but she hasn't visited our location once. She only focuses on cutting costs and doesn't care about customer service." For José, the meaning of Bobbie's behavior was a lack of customer focus. Understanding José's context was the initial step in being able to reframe.

> *Action Idea: Clarify the existing frame.* Ask potential followers to explain the context or backdrop for their interpretations of events. Funnel your questions to get at deeper layers of meaning. Keep asking the question, "What does that mean?" until you discover the specific events, behaviors, and circumstances that create the current frame.

Creating a New Level of Meaning Through Reframing

Quantum Leaders arm themselves with the knowledge of a person's existing frame to determine the degree of shared meaning. If the overlap is insufficient to attract followers, Quantum Leaders reframe the situation to change the meaning—perhaps by viewing a negative as a positive, using problems as opportunities, changing the backdrop or context of a situation, or reinterpreting a situation from a more useful perspective.

Thomas Edison reframed a tragedy that had struck his brand-new, state-of-the-art factory: a fire that burned it to the ground. Worse, Edison had no fire insurance since he had been convinced the building was fireproof. When someone commented to him that the destruction of the plant was a terrible occurrence, Edison shook his head and replied, "No, we just burned down a lot of bad ideas." Edison provided two other very powerful examples of reframing. When asked how he was able to persist during his 10,000 failures at inventing the light bulb, Edison replied that he never failed during the process; rather, he found 10,000 ways that did not work. Edison also once said, "I'm not discouraged, because every wrong attempt discarded is another step forward."

Stonewall Jackson reframed his troops' retreat during a vicious enemy attack when he said, "We're not retreating, we're advancing in a different direction." As it turned out, this was not an idle change of meaning. Jackson's strategy was to string his attackers out in line as they chased the "retreating" Union troops. Then Jackson turned his troops around and assaulted the flank of the thinly dispersed enemy lines. Jackson's reframe was necessary to inspire his troops to stay with him during the supposed retreat.

Almost any experience can be useful and worthy of support in the proper context. While I consulted with a medium-size automobile parts manufacturer, one small group of plant employees complained that a new employee was continuously on sick leave. Because of the organization's liberal policy in this area, this person continued to receive a salary and accrue other benefits. The team, which had to work very hard to meet its quotas, was disgruntled about what they perceived as an inequity.

I discussed the situation with their group supervisor, and we came up with a reframe that she agreed to try. After allowing the group to air their feelings about the issue, the supervisor explained that the company had a good health care program; if any of them got sick, their family would be provided for until they get better. She clarified that many companies do not have the substantial health care program their organization provided, and they were lucky to know that the company would take care of its employees, even new ones. The reframe caused a few heads to nod in agreement as she spoke. Then one of the longest-tenured workers said, "I guess you're right. At least we know the company cares." The reframe worked in this situation.

Managers at 3M use reframing to encourage salespeople to emphasize how their products help customers make it through a recession. Robert Hershock, a group vice-president, told *Fortune* magazine writer John Huey that he reframes the economic slowdown from a time when sales will slack off to "a real opportunity to go in and talk about the labor and cost saving aspects of our products."

Reframing also creates meaning that enables, empowers, and excites people to join with the leader and move forward together. An R&D lab's quality team leader used reframing to motivate the group to follow her lead. At one point, the group became disgruntled because they had to rework a quality proposal to include new guidelines, which would take many hours of extra work. The team captain agreed that the unexpected rework would take extra time, and that she did not even know if the new guidelines would add anything to the existing proposal. But, she added, "I also believe that with the additional effort, we can refine what we already have done to make it even better." One of the group members then spoke up: "I agree. There are some changes I would like to make to what we have, in spite of these new demands." That comment brought a strong enough wave of agreement from the rest of the group to align them behind the team captain.

In the story about José, the service company supervisor who felt that Bobbie, the new manager, did not "support the company mission," I was able to reframe the situation, with positive results. Recall that José's current frame was based on Bobbie's cost-cutting focus and the fact that she had not held any meetings with the customer service group. I suggested that perhaps Bobbie's cost-reduction efforts would ultimately serve customers; it might allow the company to reduce prices or uncover operational inefficiencies that ultimately damaged customer relations. This reframe worked for José. He asked Bobbie to meet with the customer service group and explain the cost-cutting measures. Bobbie responded positively and provided a clear presentation in which she emphasized that customer service was a high priority. The reframe had an important secondary impact because it gave José a sense of empowerment that he could create change, and feeling empowered was one of José's important core values. Reframing is more effective when it reinforces the follower's values.

Reframing Drill

Reframing is a skill that can be honed with practice. Here are some sample situations to practice on. Write out your reframe to each situation, and then compare your reframes with those listed below.

Imagine you, or those you want to lead, face the following situations and interpret them as a problem. How would you reframe them so that others will be inspired to follow?

1. Your department must trim 20 percent of its workforce.
2. Your boss wants your department to stop working on a project that the employees really enjoy.
3. Your organization has flattened its hierarchy, and twice as many people now report to you.

Here are possible reframes:

1. *Your department must trim 20 percent of its workforce* means:
   - The cutbacks give you a chance to cross-train people to enrich their jobs.
   - The rightsizing will get rid of some of the fat in your department.
   - The smaller workforce gives people a chance for more responsibility and therefore greater visibility, which should improve chances for future raises and promotions.
   - The reduction in force enables the group to rethink the way it works and develop more efficient work procedures.
   - Those who are not cut are the most valuable members of the group.
2. *Your boss wants your department to stop working on a project that the employees really enjoy* means:
   - The department can seek out other projects that are even more enjoyable.
   - The boss is finally paying close attention to you and your work, which gives you a chance to shine.
   - By your giving up this project, the boss might be willing to negotiate with you on other matters that you care about.
3. *Your organization has flattened its hierarchy, and twice as many people now report to you* means:
   - The increased staff size gives you more influence within the organization.
   - The flatter organization eliminates the miscommunication from the senior ranks.
   - You can now get approval for advanced computer technology because you need to have e-mail to make it easier for you to communicate with more people; the new technology will also be an aid to other aspects of your job.

Action Idea: Reframe one negative situation each day. To get practice, reframe a negative situation into a positive one each day. The ability to reframe a negative as a positive is critical today because of the dominance of negative news. Watch any television news show or read the front page of any paper, and you will recognize how we are bombarded with negative images. Reframe one negative situation each day to practice creating a more useful perspective.

Action Idea: Clarify the usefulness of existing frames. Effective reframes often begin by clarifying the usefulness of the follower's existing frame. For example, consider a person who states, "The company's empowerment effort has demoralized me, it has taken away the authority I worked so hard to gain over the years." An effective reframe might begin, "Yes, your situation has changed dramatically, and it is going to require a readjustment." This statement provides a match of meaning between you and the other person. You can then reframe by expanding the context of the existing frame so that the other person gains a new, more useful meaning. You could say, "You were able to make it in the old system that had so many rigid boundaries. I'm sure you will be successful in the new structure because it has fewer restrictions. In fact, you could have more influence because everyone has lost formal authority in the restructuring, but you have such good relationships with people, they will probably listen to you."

Action Idea: Affirm the negative framers. Some people tend to frame almost everything in a negative context. "Life's a pain and then you die" or "Sometimes you get the elevator, but mostly you get the shaft" are among their favorite mottos. It is difficult to respond to negative framers, but there are ways. One is to affirm the negative frame. For example, when someone complains about the difficulty of a situation, affirm the frame by saying, "Yes, it's tough, isn't it?" or "You're right; it won't be easy." The phrasing of these reframes draws the negative reframer to you because, in effect, you are matching this person's frame and thus building rapport—the sense that you and the other person are alike. With this foundation, you then might be able to suggest a reframe that is more useful and positive.

Action Idea: Reframe parts of the situation. Effective reframing sometimes requires breaking up big problems into manageable pieces. Consider what has happened to many organizations today: a drastically cut workforce, a radically restructured hierarchy, a revamped authority system, and redesigned work processes. Today's new "three R's"— rightsizing, reengineering, and restructuring—can be viewed as profanities by those who fear even more change in the workplace. Trying to reframe the meaning of all of these situations would overwhelm even the most hearty. Instead, cut the problem into small pieces, and reframe only a part of it. Refocus attention on a small area of the work redesign. Redirect people to consider one element of the new structure. A series of small reframes can build into a major transformation of meaning.

Action Idea: Reframe to bring out the sweet truth. The "sweet truth" is the meaning of an event others can easily accept. Very few people accept information that puts them in a bad light. The sweet truth points out the best side of a situation. Years ago, a shoe salesperson gave me a simple example to illustrate the power of the sweet truth. A good shoe salesperson, I was told, always tells a customer who has two different-sized feet that one foot is smaller than the other rather than that one foot is bigger. Few people want to hear they have big feet, but anyone can hear the reframe that they have a smaller foot.

Action Idea: Reframe with congruence. Reframes have to be communicated in a congruent manner. The words, tone, and nonverbal behaviors used to communicate the reframed message have to complement each other. Using a sarcastic or uninspired tone when saying, "This is really an opportunity," will not garner much followership. Giving a disapproving or condescending glance when saying, "I'm sure you're going to find this beneficial," sends a mixed message that limits the potential for shared meaning. Leon Moore's reframe about how excited he was to work for the IRS was totally congruent. He was standing straight, smiling broadly, his eyes bright with enthusiasm, and his tone upbeat.

Manipulation or Motivation: Humpty-Dumpty Talk

I once overheard someone giving advice about how to manipulate others. The person said, "Sincerity is the secret. You say whatever you have to to prove that you are sincere." Reframing can be used to manipulate information in the worst sense, or frame, of the word *manipulation*. Some people reframe information to gain followers when they do not have the followers' best interests at heart. I call this Humpty-Dumpty talk, based on Humpty-Dumpty's comment, "When I use a word, it means what I choose it to mean—nothing more, nothing less." I do not consider manipulation to be Quantum Leader reframing (that is my reframe!).

Humpty-Dumpty talk is the spin control politicians use. A joke about Washington politicos is that a political rival is slick when the rival can fool the public more successfully than the opponent can. Spin control in the culture of Washington, D.C., helps people merely look and sound good in the image they project rather than demonstrate that they are successful. In business, Humpty-Dumpty talk avoids substance in favor of form or to mask what is going on. One of the explanations suggested as contributing to General Motors's decline from a premier auto manufacturer to an industry dinosaur was the use of slick accounting procedures. According to this account in *Rude Awakening* by Maryann Keller, GM executives toiled endlessly to present their numbers in the most favorable light. Those who got ahead in the organization were not creating value; rather, they had the greatest talent for sprucing up their balance sheets to simply look good.

Humpty-Dumpty talk creates blame rather than presents a frame that solves a problem. Humpty-Dumpty talk is also the hype spewed by advertisers to hawk a product. When we hear, "new and improved," "100 percent natural," and "low in sodium, fat, and cholesterol," we realize that advertisers are often simply hyping their product news for marketing purposes rather than signaling substantive changes.

Quantum Leaders recognize the potential misuse of reframing; they know that they control the intention to manipulate, misguide, mask, or otherwise mislead. Because the value of reframing is to create shared meaning with followers, they do not abuse the process with Humpty-Dumpty talk.

When Reframing Will Not Work

Reframes might not work for three reasons. First, a reframe may fail when it suggests a meaning too far afield from the follower's existing frame. For example, almost any reframe will fail to convince a strong pro-choice person that abortion is murder. Similarly, no frame will influence a strong right-to-life proponent that abortion is a woman's right.

Reframes may also fail if they lack elegance, that is, they do not offer a compelling new meaning for the situation. A manager in a computer company that was experiencing low sales revenues but was also backlogged with work bungled an attempt to influence his boss when he reframed the need for more staff by saying, "We would be helping the local economy by hiring more people."

The third reason that reframing may not have impact stems from a lack of trust. When I hear a person say, "I don't care how it sounds, I don't believe that guy," I know the reframe may be elegant, but the person will not follow because of a lack of trust. Strained relationships result in rejected reframes. Without some degree of trust and common ground, possible followers mock the reframe because they perceive it as a manipulative ploy or insincere attempt to change the followers' minds about an issue. In this situation, no leadership occurs. The quality of leader-follower relationships is an important foundation of Quantum Leadership, and it has a direct impact on reframing.

"Wet-Finger-in-the-Air" Leadership

Matching followers' values and frames of reference does not mean leaders simply guide the followers where the followers already want to go. Quantum Leaders do not practice "wet-finger-in-the-air" leadership: holding a finger in the air to test the direction of the wind and then pointing in that direction. Quantum Leadership transcends simply telling people what they want to hear.

The Quantum Leader performs enlightened action while engaging the full power of the Quantum Leader within. The intention is to make a difference, not to assume the posture of the sycophant. The Quantum Leader's attention focuses on ways to overcome difficulties and exploit opportunities that realize meaningful results, not merely to pander for followers. The Quantum Leader's discrimination creates choices, selects options, and takes initiatives designed to inspire, motivate, and produce beneficial outcomes rather than to gain popular support.

10

Influence Strategies

"If we want to be heard we must speak in a language the listener can understand and on a level at which the listener is capable of operating."

—M. Scott Peck, *author of* The Road Less Traveled

Have you ever tried to convince someone to do something but just could not get through? Even though your direction was in line with their values (you thought) and you provided a useful and attractive frame of reference, he or she still resisted your direction. While values and frames of reference are two methods Quantum Leaders use to create shared meaning, they also understand and rely on more subtle strategies to perform enlightened action and attract followers. These persuasion strategies are designed to match the way followers structure information in their consciousness.

Internal Information Processing Codes:
Private Mental Languages

People use specific internal codes or modalities to portray experiences in their minds. For example, some people portray experiences visually: They actually *see* pictures. Others make sense of information auditorily: They literally represent information by *sound.* Still others process information kinesthetically: They create meaning as *feelings.*

Internal information processing codes are the subtlest level at which people assign meaning to their experience. Unlike values and frames of reference, internal information processing codes are the fundamental routines that define how people take in, sort, store, access, and configure "raw data." They are similar to codes used by Western Union operators to make sense of the telegraph line beeps.

Internal information processing codes form a person's private mental language. For example, visuals who are detail-oriented have to see every fact, figure, and bit of information available, because they do not notice or know how to recognize generalities very well. Quantum Leader influence means speaking the follower's private mental language. People learn their internal language, just as they learn English, Spanish, or Japanese. Because only a finite number exist, Quantum Leaders can learn the internal codes and then create an overlap of meaning that attracts committed followers by speaking their private mental language.

Four key internal codes form the foundation of the private mental languages people use to create meaning:

1. Visual/auditory/kinesthetic code
2. Approach/avoidance code
3. Similarity/difference code
4. Detail/generality code

Understanding the Visual/Auditory/Kinesthetic Code

The visual/auditory/kinesthetic (VAK) code reveals that some people create meaning as pictures, others as sounds, and still others as feelings or actions. It is important to know that everyone uses a combination of VAK, and none is more effective than another. Visual, auditory, and kinesthetic are simply different ways to structure information. However, many people rely more heavily on one of the three.

Visual people want to "see" what you mean or "get a good picture," and they "show" you things to make them "perfectly clear." Things "look good" or "look bad" to them. Ideas may "appear insightful," or they may be "hazy" or "foggy."

Auditory people like to be "told," and they want you to "listen." They "hear" you when things "sound good," "purr like a kitten," and "ring a bell." They do not "tune in" when you "sound" bad or "blabber."

Kinesthetic people want to "get moving," "take a step," and "hang in there" when things are "rough" or "hard to handle." They "get close," "catch on," and "walk hand in hand" when they follow, but they "slip away" or do not want the "hassle" when they choose not to follow.

In order to recognize visuals, Quantum Leaders attend to words and phrases and observe physical actions. They pay attention to typical phrases, such as "a dim view," "the naked eye," "plainly see," and "the image," and look for steady eye contact as indicators of visual people. They know that visual people usually look directly at things to understand them. It is common for a visual person to peek into your office, look over your shoulder, or request to see documents or other materials.

Quantum Leaders tune in to auditory types when they hear typical comments such as "hold your tongue," "listen up," "give me an earful," and "explain it word for word." Auditory people often turn their ear toward a speaker. They may even cup their ear while listening intently. They do not need to make eye contact when talking to someone and, in fact, may close their eyes while listening, which heightens their hearing ability. An auditory person likes to use the telephone and will have long conversations. Some IBM executives might have responded better to CEO Lou Gerstner had they understood that he probably has a strong preference for the auditory mode. According to a story in Paul Carroll's *Big Blues: The Unmaking of IBM*, Gerstner forbade executives from using overhead slides, insisting that if somebody had something to say, he or she should just say it.

Quantum Leaders catch on to kinesthetic people by typical comments such as "touch base," "point out," "turn things around," "get my mind around it," "control it," and "all washed up." Kinesthetic types like to make physical contact: shake hands or touch an arm or shoulder, pick up objects and feel their texture, or rub their hands together without the need to warm them. They often stretch in meetings, run their hands along a table, or tap on objects.

Action Idea: Pay attention to VAK words and phrases. Watch for visual words and phrases such as *see, look, watch, eyeful, clearly, from my point of view, image, hindsight, focused, catch a glimpse,* or *make a scene.* Listen attentively for auditory words and phrases such as *soft, idle talk, to tell the truth, hear, amplify, tune in/out, be all ears, rings a bell,* or *manner of speaking.* Tap into kinesthetic words and phrases such as *make contact, get a hold of, catch on, turn around, concrete, smooth out, come to grips with, control yourself, firm foundation, get the drift, keep your shirt on, pull some strings,* or *too much of a hassle.*

Action Idea: Pay attention to greetings and goodbyes. Greetings and goodbyes offer fertile ground for understanding VAK codes. Visual types look at you and remark, "Nice to see you" or "You're looking great," and maintain eye contact when they leave, commenting, "I'll see you again." Auditory types greet you by saying, "I'm glad to speak to you" or "It's great to talk to you again," say goodbye by telling you that "it was great to hear from you" and "I'll call you soon." Kinesthetic people often greet others by shaking their hands or touching their arms. Kinesthetic types comment that "it feels so good to be in touch," and when they part, they might say, "Keep in touch," as they shake your hand again or make some other physical contact.

Action Idea: Ask questions. To understand VAK, ask, "What is your experience regarding . . . ?" The question is neutral since the word *experience* can apply to V, A, or K. The response to the question usually reveals how the person processes information. For example, one manager responded to the question, "What is your experience regarding the recent downsizing?" by saying, "Things look pretty grim now. You can see by the looks on people's faces that they have a dim view of what happened." This manager was clearly a visual type.

Action Idea: Pay attention to the VAK sequence. Since in reality everyone uses all three elements of this code, they typically use VAK in a sequence or syntax. Some may hear, see, then feel; others feel, hear, then see. Pay attention to the VAK syntax to expand your capacity to understand and match people's private mental language. Consider this statement: "Look, I don't see how this will happen. It's really frustrating to me. I feel my hands are tied. What can you tell me?" The sequence of these statements is V, then K, then A—crucial to the particular sequence of the person's internal language.

Action Idea: Watch the eyes. Richard Bandler and John Grinder pioneered neurolinguistic programming (NLP), the science of internal information processing codes. They explain in their book, *Frogs into Princes,* that people look up when they see information in their minds; people look to their right or left, level with their ears, or down and to their left when they subliminally hear information; and people look down and to their lower right when they are accessing information kinesthetically.

Understanding the Approach/Avoidance Code

The approach/avoidance code is concerned with how people represent information in terms of either what they want to experience (approach) or what they do not want to experience (avoidance). This internal meaning creation code stems from the desire for comfort and the dislike of pain. People who represent information in the approach mode structure reality by "moving toward" something in order to realize more pleasure and to minimize pain. The statement, "I really want to get home early tonight," indicates the approach person moving forward. People who represent information in the avoidance mode structure information by "moving away" to experience less pain and more pleasure. An avoidance person might say, "I hope I don't get home late tonight." Both aim for the same thing—more comfort, less discomfort—but their internal code structures a different reality for each.

Everyone uses a combination of approach and avoidance, but most people consistently favor one or the other. A vice president of human resources recently said to me, "I believe the new employee assistance program will help our people feel better about the company" (an approach interpretation); another vice president in the same company remarked that the same employee assistance program "should limit the potential for employees to make claims that the company is unfair" (an avoidance interpretation). The first vice president wanted a new human resources management software package to help analyze data more easily. The second wanted the same package to help minimize errors that might create problems with employee records. The approach vice president attended association meetings as a way to network and build credibility within the industry. The avoidance vice president attended the same meetings because he did not want his boss to think he was not a committed career person.

Avoidance may appear as a negative, unproductive mode; however, avoidance can be beneficial. An avoidance person can be very useful when considering ways to minimize losses or to avoid problems. People who move away from a lit match do not get burned.

Quantum Leaders notice the approach/avoidance code by carefully attending to people's language, logic, and explanations for behavior.

Action Idea: Pay attention to approach/avoidance language. To recognize approach people, learn to identify language that indicates moving toward something or phrases that suggest an attempt to gain something. Use the same attention power to identify avoidance people's statements about what they do not want to happen or do not want to lose.

Action Idea: Ask questions to determine approach/avoidance. Ask questions such as, "What do you want from your job?" or "What do you want from the company?" Approach people will tell you what they want; avoiders will tell you what they do not want.

Action Idea: Notice situational approach/avoidance. Some people may be approach oriented in some situations and avoidance oriented in others. A tax lawyer I know uses avoidance when it comes to dealing with the IRS; she wants to stay away from the possibility of an audit. Yet she slips into the approach mode when she considers entertainment; she rock-climbs and hang-glides to seek excitement.

Understanding the Similarity/Difference Code

The third internal code creates meaning in terms of similarities and differences. Similarity people make comments such as, "This is just like the last one" or "We did this yesterday," because they process information as commonalities. Difference people say, "It's completely different from what we did before," or, "I've never done anything like this," because their private mental language forms meanings as contrasts.

The similarity/difference code has two subcodes: People can interpret exceptions to a similarity, or they can interpret exceptions to a difference. In the first case, they may comment, "They are all the same size, except this one, which is a little larger." In the second case, they may comment, "Every one of these is a different size, except these two, which are the same." People can switch around among the four variations of this code depending on the situation, but most favor one of the four.

Quantum Leaders notice the similarity/difference code and its two subcodes when people describe how they compare things and how they make distinctions about events.

> *Action Idea: Pay attention to similarity/difference comments.* Listen for statements that reveal the general code, "It's all the same" or "It's all different," and attend to comments that reveal one or the other subcode based on exceptions: "These are all the [same/different] except this one."

> *Action Idea: Ask questions to determine similarity/difference.* Ask, "How do these [objects/events/people] compare?" or "What is the relationship between these [objects/events/people]?" The answers offer insight into which code people favor.

Understanding the Detail/Generality Code

The fourth internal code reveals that some people create meaning in the form of details, while others favor a general overview to interpret information. Detail people make presentations using specific facts and figures. They read everything, and they examine the fine print because to them, every bit of information is important. Detail people review information again and again so that they do not miss any point of information. In contrast, when generality people give a briefing, they emphasize only "what's important." They make a few short statements about "the highlights," which they feel tell the entire story. They need only an overview of the main points to understand information. When they pick up a book or a report, they review only summary graphs and charts. They feel that a quick, cursory inspection of situations gives them the whole story. When the human resources manager in a large corporation wants to review a new training program, he slips into the back of the room for 10 to 15 minutes. He claims, "That's all the time I need to know if the program is worthwhile for us."

Although people can use both elements of this code, most tend to be more comfortable with one or the other, and they continue to make meaning using their dominant mode.

Quantum Leaders recognize this code by noticing how much information people request and by observing how people respond to the information they are given.

Action Idea: Pay attention to requests. Requests such as, "Do you have any more information?" "What did it cost?" or "Can you give me some background?" reflect the detail mode. Generality requests include, "What is the bottom line?" "Do you have a summary chart?" or "Tell me the one thing that is most important."

Action Idea: Notice how people handle written material. Detail people carefully review almost all of the written material they are given. They take lots of notes. A document returned from a detail person will be well handled (many folded pages, lots of dog-eared corners, and generally worn-looking paper). Generality people read the summary or table of contents, perhaps underlining just one or two items. A document read by a generality person will remain in pristine shape (few creases, no marks, only one or two pages handled).

Action Idea: Ask questions designed to reveal detail vs. general response. Ask, "What do you need to know about this?" and "How will you know if you understand this?" The detail person will reply, "Well, I'll have to go over all the numbers and get some background reports." The generality person will retort, "I'll know after I see the total cost" or "It will be obvious if I get the most important points."

Speaking the Follower's Private Mental Language

Quantum Leaders gain entry into the follower's private mental language by recognizing which internal codes are used. Quantum Leader influence occurs when they speak the follower's language or match his or her internal codes to create shared meaning.

Matching another person's private mental language is like speaking his or her native tongue. We easily understand that people who are raised to speak Spanish think and talk in Spanish, just as people from Germany think and talk in German, and people raised in Japan represent their world in Japanese. We quickly realize how hard it is to communicate with people who speak a language that we do not know. We believe that if we speak Spanish, we can easily communicate shared meaning when Spanish is the native tongue, and we certainly think that we can communicate with English-speaking people if we speak English. However, the subtle, internal codes that make up our private mental language also have to be matched to create the powerful quantum influence connection of shared meaning.

Jay Stark Thompson, CEO of Life Technologies, a supplier of tools to life sciences researchers, understands the need to match the private mental language of others. According to Faye Rice, writing for *Fortune* magazine (June 3, 1991), Thompson states, "I've learned that just because you think it, write it, or say it doesn't mean employees hear it or believe it." Thompson explains that a graphic picture or image may be required, or a behavioral portrait might be needed to get across the meaning of an idea. Thompson also understands that internal codes must be matched individually. That is, he discounts general exhortations such as "achieve better quality." Thompson favors talking directly to shop workers to hammer home the importance of sending precisely correct amounts of chemicals in every vial leaving the factory.

Matching internal codes requires the attention power of the Quantum Leader within. Quantum Leaders pay attention to the signals that indicate each of the codes; then they use their discrimination to recognize subtle private mental language differences and to discern when people switch modes, such as an auditory person who suddenly wants to be shown a direction. Quantum Leaders are intent on matching the follower's private mental language and take initiative to do so.

Matching the VAK Pattern

Quantum Leaders match the follower's VAK code by showing the visual people, telling the auditory types, and making contact with the kinesthetic people.

> *Action Idea: Make pictures for the visual person.* Use visual language such as *see, look, glimpse* and create mental pictures to match visual people. Show them pictures, graphs, or charts. Draw sketches for them when you explain your points. Create visual presentations using video or computer imagery. Match the visual person by using colors and bright light. Let the visual person see what you are doing or writing. Make eye contact, and use facial expressions to support your ideas. Adjust your eyebrows in concert with your ideas. And smile. Visual people see the smile, and you probably look better to them that way.

> *Action Idea: Make it sound good for the auditory person.* Match auditory people with language that rings a bell for them. Use words such as *tell, hear,* and *listen* to create a resounding sense of shared meaning. Adjust your tone to emphasize key words. Speak clearly, and adjust your rate of speech to theirs. Repeat words and phrases that reinforce what you want. Restate the words auditory types say to reinforce that you have heard them.

> *Action Idea: Get in touch with the kinesthetic person.* Allow the kinesthetic people to hold on to a document or other object that is relevant to your point. Firmly shake hands with them when appropriate. Use kinesthetic phrases such

as *grab on, smooth sailing,* and *solid ground* to match meaning. Emphasize feelings with statements such as, "I get the feeling . . ." and "This is going to be tough, but we can get through it."

Action Idea: Match the VAK syntax. Match the person's VAK syntax by adopting his or her sequence of VAK elements. If the person "tells you how they feel" (A-K syntax) respond by "saying how you feel." If the person "sees that it rings a chord," (V-A syntax) match them by "showing them you are listening."

Matching the Approach/Avoidance Code

Quantum Leaders match approach people by explaining what they will gain by following and avoidance people by ensuring them they will not have to experience specific outcomes if they follow the leader.

Action Idea: Point out how "moving toward" benefits the approachers. Match approach people with statements such as, "You're really going to gain if you do . . . ," or "You will benefit in this way if you go in this direction," or "By taking this path, you will receive this positive result."

Action Idea: Clarify how no harm will come to avoiders. Match avoidance people with comments such as, "You can avert that danger by doing . . . ," or "It will be worse unless you do . . . ," or "When you take this path, you won't have to deal with . . ."

Matching the Similarity/Difference Code

Quantum Leaders match similarity people by emphasizing correspondences. They match similarity-with-exception people by asserting the larger degree of similarity and agreeing to the portion that is different. Matching difference people requires some finesse. By definition, if you match them, they might find a difference that then cracks your attempt to create shared meaning.

Action Idea: Point out similarities. Say, "This is just like what we did last week," or, "Notice that the changes are almost identical to what happened last week and we made it through that," or "Everything here compares very well with the other program."

Action Idea: Clarify similarities with exceptions. Say, "You can see that every one of these requests is almost identical, and this unique one won't be hard to deal with," or, "I know this part doesn't fit, but the rest of this is all the same."

Action Idea: Allow similarity people to build on your lead. Similarity people usually reinforce your lead because they will try to find something they can recognize and accept. Match the similarity mode by asking, "What more would you do to get us moving in this direction?" or "How can we make this initiative more effective?" A similarity person will often respond, "I recognize a way to do it."

Action Idea: Ask for differences. Ask difference people, "What's different about this?" or "Does this appear unlike what we have done before?" Difference people will chime in with the many contrasts they notice. Simply asking for difference reinforces their interpretation, which creates rapport because you demonstrate that you understand their private mental language.

Action Idea: Appreciate the difference person. Difference people find it hard to get along with others because they disagree so often. By focusing on discrepancies, difference people distance themselves from others. One way to create shared meaning with them is to thank them for their contributions and to acknowledge the validity of their insights. Appreciating difference people *because* they see difference bonds them to you.

Action Idea: Acknowledge the difference and ask for support. When difference people counter your lead, openly acknowledge it: "Yes, that is a difference." Be silent for a few moments. Then ask for their support. The purpose here is twofold. First, difference people may reverse themselves by saying, "Well, it might not be that different," and then support your lead. This sounds somewhat unrealistic, but I have experienced it, it can work. Second, by agreeing with difference people, you join them at their level of meaning. That connection may establish enough overlap of meaning to influence them to follow.

Action Idea: Rely on matching other internal codes. The tricky nature of matching difference people might be circumvented by focusing on their VAK code or their detail/generality code as a way to create shared meaning.

Matching the Detail/Generality Code

Quantum Leaders match detail people with mounds of data, facts, and statistics and match generality people with overviews, summaries, and bottom-line statements.

Action Idea: Rely on others to help you match detail and generality people. It is easy to match detail people if you are one yourself, and you can easily talk generality people's language if you are also a big-picture person. Matching your opposite can be difficult. One way is to rely on others to help you create a match. For example, if you have to give a report to a detail person and you can think of only two main points, find a detail person and ask that person for help in developing an itemized package of information. Similarly, find a general person to help you if you are a detail person.

The Quantum Reality of Matching Internal Codes

Internal codes represent broad categories that people use to create meaning. The way any particular follower makes meaning of any single bit of information cannot be absolutely determined. Human information processing has great flexibility. Uncertainty and probabilities govern this subtle layer of life. Human consciousness can take a quantum leap and change from one code to another. A generality person might suddenly say, "I need more information. Let's get into some of the specific numbers," after you have prepared only a short general overview of financial data. An auditory person might pop out with, "Haven't you got anything I can look at? I need to see this more clearly," after you have outlined everything you thought the person needed to hear.

Speaking the follower's private mental language requires experimentation. Quantum Leaders accept the risk associated with trying to influence others *(the sixth natural law of leadership)*. They thrive on the challenge because of their intention to lead. They keep their attention sharply focused to recognize a change in the use of any code. And they increase their discrimination by preparing more response choices: They may develop a well-articulated speech, prepare several eye-catching graphs, and bring materials that followers can leaf through or hold to reach all the VAK modes. They can explain how their direction will create possibilities and assure how following will minimize problems. Quantum Leaders know how to create comparisons, and they are ready to acknowledge and accept the existence of differences. Finally, Quantum Leaders prepare to communicate their direction with both an executive summary and many pages of charts and graphs. The better the match is, the greater is the possibility that their action will create shared meaning and enlighten others to support their leader initiative.

Quantum Leader influence, creating shared meaning, and performing enlightened action change the follower's consciousness by connecting at the follower's level, then guiding the follower to the leader's level of consciousness. Despite the best efforts, it is not always possible to change follower consciousness. *The seventh natural law of leadership* states that not everyone will follow a leader. When people are locked into a particular state of awareness, it may be very difficult and extremely time-consuming to gain their commitment.

Quantum Leaders also know that they can increase the probability of influencing people to follow by cultivating relationships that create a sense of common ground, trust, and credibility. By developing the relationship foundation, Quantum Leaders strengthen the impact of performing enlightened action.

11

Leader-Quality Relationships

"No matter how busy you are, you must take time to make the other person feel important."

—*Mary Kay Ash, founder of Mary Kay Cosmetics*

Quantum Leaders do not attract followers in a vacuum. Leaders and followers typically have a relationship history outside the events that bond them together in a Quantum Leadership field. People socialize together during and after work, and they interact when they work together. Good relationships create meaningful bonds. Awkward, uncomfortable, and negative interactions, in contrast, distance people. Association can breed respect, and it can create contempt.

The Quantum Leadership model shows that the quality of interpersonal relationships forms the foundation of the Quantum Leader–follower interaction (Figure 11-1). This relationship establishes a platform that will either support or fail to support the leader's initiatives. Quantum Leaders realize that people are more likely to respond to their call for support when people hold the leader in high regard and are already on their leader's side.

Garry Nelson, a senior partner at the executive search firm

Figure 11-1. The Quantum Leadership model: The relationship foundation.

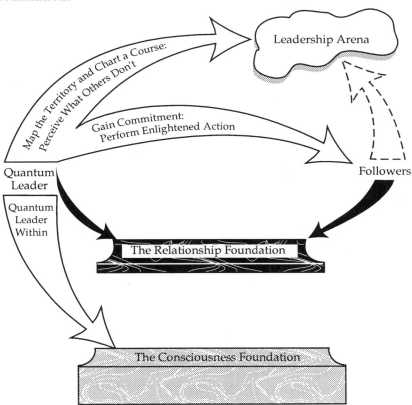

Rhodes Associates, made developing positive relationships with others a number one priority throughout his twenty-year career as a senior human resource specialist in several large financial institutions and insurance companies. When he took his first corporate position, Nelson explained, "If I can't connect with the people I'm working with and let them know we're in this together, they're not going to listen to what I have to say. I'll have little influence if I don't establish positive interactions with people."

Nelson's insight may sound like simple common sense. But as Will Rogers once said, "Common sense ain't so common." Many people, even highly skilled individuals, can forget or overlook the primary importance of relationship building. For example, Jimmy Carter failed to create important alliances with power brokers within the D.C. beltway when he assumed the presidency in 1976. Carter relied heavily on his "Georgia Mafia," a limited field of relationships with home state cronies. He never established the necessary bonds with the players of national politics in Washington to create a more expanded field necessary for presidential leadership in Washington, D.C. Despite Carter's dedication to his office and his highly regarded intellect, his limited interactions and strained relationships hampered his presidency.

The capacity to influence others beyond the dictates of formal authority rests heavily on the quality of relationship. Many leader initiatives fail when this fundamental reality is violated. A study by Morgan McCall and Michael Lombardo in *Psychology Today* in 1983, identified ten factors that caused high-potential executives to derail their career success. The top three reasons were insensitivity to others—abrasive, intimidating, bullying style; cold, aloof, arrogant behavior; and betrayal of trust. Think of your own experience. How do you react to a call for support from a person you do trust? What response do you typically give to someone's initiative when you have a negative impression of the person?

Quantum Leaders know that good relationships do not simply happen, and they cultivate leader-quality relationships—interactions that increase the probability of gaining followers. Four areas are particularly important here:

1. Establish a common ground.
2. Provide valued resources.
3. Develop trust.
4. Build credibility.

Establish a Common Ground

Lou Hughes, the president of General Motors Europe, learned German to communicate with local hourly workers. He immersed himself in the language for six months and required colleagues to use it in meetings with him. Hughes is now so competent that he uses German even in conversation with English-speaking Germans. At the Minnesota headquarters of Toro, the lawnmower and snow blower company, CEO Kendrick Melrose tries to eat lunch at least once a month with employees. He puts in occasional sessions on the assembly line, and answers customer service telephones. Every quarter F. H. Behrendt, CEO of Exabyte, the computer tape-drive producer, meets for two and a half hours with all employees for questions and answers. He introduces new employees, shows slides of them, and says something personal and interesting about each. All three demonstrate ways to cultivate a common ground.

When leaders and followers stand together on a platform of shared experience and understanding, they share a common ground that transforms individual separateness into a holistic field of interaction. With a common ground, individual consciousness becomes unified, collective consciousness, like disparate energy waves that join to form a new, coherent wave.

A common ground connects the Quantum Leader with other people's subjective views of reality so that the leader can look through their eyes and listen with their ears. Retired army general Norman Schwarzkopf admits that he is an impatient man, yet he understood the need to establish a common ground with the Saudi royal family during the Persian Gulf crisis. Schwarzkopf spent endless hours philosophizing with the family members because that was *their* way of making decisions.

A common ground creates a meeting of the minds and a joining of the hearts. When people are like each other, they usually like each other. A common ground develops when people share the same background, compatible interests, or similar goals. Even a common geography can create an immediate common ground. During the introductions to my seminars and speaking engagements, I often mention that I have lived in Santa Barbara, New York, and Boston, and in the midwestern states of Ohio, Indiana, Illinois, Oklahoma, and Iowa. During breaks, many people say: "You know, I lived in Iowa too," or "Where did you live in Indiana? I grew up there," or "My son goes to school in Santa Barbara; I really like it there." Furthermore, because I travel a good deal, I can usually create a common bond by referring to places where people grew up that I have visited. During a program I conducted in Denver, a manager explained that he was raised in Oregon near the Columbia River gorge. Two weeks earlier, I had conducted a retreat in that area for a senior management group. When I described my experience of the majestic countryside, the manager and I made an immediate connection.

Developing a Common Ground

Developing a common ground with others involves three basic steps:

1. Make the B.I.G. connection: Learn about the other person's *b*ackground, *i*nterests, and *g*oals.
2. Identify the shared aspect of your experience.
3. Accept people as they are.

The B.I.G. Connection: Learn About the Person

Quantum Leaders take a conscious interest in the background, interests, and goals of others, listening to what people talk about, asking questions, and observing the surroundings to learn more. They identify those individuals with whom they need to develop better relationships.

Action Idea: Conduct a "stranger audit." A "stranger audit" will help assess the quality of your relationships and degree of common ground with specific people. Common ground requires a sense of interpersonal comfort, the feeling of being at ease with another person, and the sense of being glad to be with another person. People rarely follow a person if they feel uncomfortable or "strange" around that person. You need to know how much "strangeness" exists between yourself and others as a first step in minimizing discomfort and maximizing your chances for gaining willing followers.

Figure 11-2 is an example of a completed stranger audit. To conduct your own stranger audit, prepare a similar grid, listing the people's names down the grid's left side. Then rate each person on your list in terms of how comfortable you feel around him or her, using the scale along the grid's top, with 1 equaling very uncomfortable and 10 equaling very comfortable. My experience is that the extent to which you feel comfortable around others is a fair indication of how comfortable they feel around you.

Figure 11-2. The stranger audit.

Names	Very Uncomfortable 1	2	3	4	5	6	7	8	Very Comfortable 9	10
Terry										X
Ronnie			X							
Clive						X				
Dick										X
Marlena								X		
Jim										X
Davis	X									
Rubio						X				
Paula										X
Buddy		X								

Make your rankings using what I call the "gut check" technique. What is your gut reaction response to the question: "How comfortable do I feel about this person?" After completing your rankings, think about those people whom you rank below a 5. These are the "strangers" you need to work with to build a common ground. Conduct stranger audits regularly.

Action Idea: Learn one fact about someone each day. Discover new information about people's work background, educational history, professional likes and dislikes, career interests and aspirations, non-job-related hobbies, preferences regarding food, cars, or vacations, and their future hopes and expectations. People often take it for granted that they "know all about" another person, when in reality they usually know very little about the person's background, interests, and goals. Daily fact finding breaks through the boundary of limited knowledge.

Action Idea: Observe artifacts. The artifacts in a person's office often provide powerful clues to their interests. Alex Stolley, while CEO of Northlich Stolley, a Cincinnati-based advertising agency, had pictures of airplanes on the wall and a small model airplane on his desk. These artifacts were not accidental. Stolley was an avid aviator who piloted his own plane on weekends. A question about artifacts offers an effective way to connect with someone. Alex Stolley loved to talk about flying.

Action Idea: Allow small steps. Accept that some people will disclose information to you in small steps. Let them work at their pace until they feel safe enough to reveal more.

Action Idea: Respect the boundaries of personal disclosure. People usually have boundaries surrounding their willingness to make personal disclosures. Some people feel uncomfortable talking about their private lives or view such information as inappropriate workplace conversation. Some people might not be too open about revealing information about professional hopes, aspirations, and interests because of a concern about how their motivations might be interpreted. Respect the preference for confidentiality. The president of a privately owned company I know does not like to talk about himself or his professional experiences; however, he does have a passionate interest in his company and its activities. We connect by talking about our mutual interest in developing his organization's competitive excellence.

Action Idea: Disclose important facts about yourself. Self-disclosure begets self-disclosure. Disclose important facts about yourself to every person on your staff on a regular basis. Your openness can set the stage for others to reciprocate.

Action Idea: Take a ride in a pickup. Floyd Hoelting, director of residence life at Illinois State University, takes people for rides in his '52 Chevy pickup when he wants to establish a common ground. Floyd adores his dented old pickup. It rides like a bucking bronco, but it is perfect for getting around on Floyd's ranch. Emblazoned on the pickup doors in big red letters is "Floyd Hoelting, Professional Auctioneer," an avocation that he loves to demonstrate! When you go for a ride in his pickup, you enter Floyd's world. He allows you to become one with him. While jostling down the road in that pickup, Floyd spontaneously tells stories about himself, his family, and his dreams; his interest in horses and cattle; his love for the outdoors; and his belief that people need to share a sense of community. Floyd's openness naturally warms others to talk about themselves. A ride in Floyd's pickup is a perfect place for him to build relationships with others.

What is the comparable pickup truck in your life?

Where can you take people to let them know about you and what you value, thus setting a stage for them to talk about themselves? Find that place, activity, or vehicle, and invite people into it.

Identify the Shared Aspect of Your Experience

Armed with the knowledge of another's interests, backgrounds, intents, and goals, Quantum Leaders seek to identify the shared aspect of experience that creates the common ground. In some cases, this is easy. When I meet someone who enjoys traveling, likes baseball, or studies physics as a hobby, we immediately share an interest. In other cases, finding the shared aspect of experience requires some digging.

Fred, a manager in a large chemical plant, plays tennis almost every day. Tennis is such a part of his life that he translates his work experiences into a tennis game. Interactions with others are "matches" in which he "serves" ideas and then "returns" information to others. Fred subscribes to several tennis magazines, and his office is littered with tennis paraphernalia. "Getting the ball over the net" consumes Fred's life. In contrast, I have whacked a ball over a net a few times in my life, but I do not really count that as playing tennis, so I had to work to create a common ground with this tennis buff. I like sports, but for Fred, tennis *is* sports, so that did not draw us together. I am interested in coaching, for sports and as a tool for managers to develop job-related skills. One day I asked Fred to explain how he improved his tennis game. He told me about his tennis lessons and described the teaching videos he watched. My focus on the fine points of coaching has established a common ground of interests that helped solidify our relationship.

Action Idea: Point out the shared experience. Tell people directly what you have in common. This may sound too elementary even to mention, yet I have known people who do not clarify common interests because they think it is not important. For six months, I consulted with a production vice president and his six-person quality team. Two of the team members were attending night school to get advanced degrees. The vice president had attended the same program at the same school several years earlier, but he never mentioned it despite the many discussions the entire team had about the program. The vice president explained to me, "Well, that isn't relevant to producing results in our quality effort." One reason I was brought in to consult with this group was that the relationships with the vice president and his group were strained.

Action Idea: Identify areas of experience overlap. When you do not share any specific experience with someone, you may have to look for an overlap area. Fred's interest in developing his tennis game overlapped with my interest in coaching. At times, establishing the overlap may be less direct. I worked with a man from a large wholesale food distributor who was marketing vice president of fat and oil food products. He had graduated from college with a chemistry degree and before he joined the wholesale food company had worked for a chemical plant that produced food products. I had done work with a chemical plant that produced polypropylene, the plastic-based material used in food-related substances. When I talked about my experience at the plastics plant operation and we found the production processes used in both plants had some similarities, I discovered an overlap area for us to establish an initial common point of relationship. Seek related information from people to find overlap areas of experience. Offer information that appears to be connected as a means to introduce a common ground.

Accept People as They Are

When someone is already like us, it is easy to identify with and accept them. We bond easily with people in the fertile soil of ground we already occupy. The process becomes tougher with those who differ from us on important issues.

Quantum Leaders work at accepting people as they are. They transcend the boundaries that separate them to operate from a more unified sense of their relationship with others. They recognize the quantum field reality that, at some deep level of life, they are not separate from anything they experience. They consciously self-refer back to the source level of consciousness, pure consciousness, that dissolves the self versus other distinctions. From this state, Quantum Leaders can accept others with honor and respect, not judgment.

> *Action Idea: Honor a difference as simply one frame of reference.* The quantum paradigm reveals that reality is subjective, based in consciousness. Differences are frames of reference. Honor the different interest, background, or point of view of another person as one frame of reality. You do not have to agree with the frame for yourself; you only need to accept it as a frame that works for the person from the person's level of consciousness. The act of acceptance forges the possibility for a common ground because it demonstrates an openness to the person.

> *Action Idea: Practice nonjudgmental acceptance with one person each day.* Resolve to listen and accept whatever you are told by one person each day. Naturally you want to pick your spots carefully with this choice. At first, try this action idea in a nonbusiness-related context so that you do not compromise yourself in a bottom-line situation.

> *Action Idea: Dance at the other person's rhythm.* It is hard to establish a common ground when we are so busy protecting our own point of view. We cannot or will not seek to unite points of view if we must always defend our position to the exclusion of others. Quantum Leaders maintain their beliefs and preferences but also seek ways to get into step with another person, much like two dancers seeking

a common rhythm. Practice letting go of your point of view as a means to get in touch with the other person's perspective.

It's Not My Style

Some people type themselves as introverts and lament that their style limits their capacity to find and share interests. Introverts feel uncomfortable with relationship building that requires sharing information about themselves or seeking information about others. More gregarious people usually can find it easier to try the action ideas that suggest getting to know others. Yet introverts too can improve their skills in this area.

For those who feel "it's not my style," create a structure for your common ground-building activities. Make specific appointments, attend scheduled activities, and set agendas for yourself to cultivate a common ground. Relationship building typically does not happen by itself for those who prefer to be introverts, but a structure can help the process.

Action Idea: Double your face-to-face contact rate. Double your face-to-face contact rate to structure getting out and talking to people. Set aside time every week with each person in your area. Create a one-month action plan for face-to-face contact, and stick to it.

Action Idea: Create an interaction space near your office. An interaction space is a place where people can congregate comfortably for a few minutes during the day. Creating such a place near your office draws people to you, which makes it easier to break out of the introversion tendency. The interaction space also saves time because going out to visit others requires an investment of time. One manager placed a popcorn machine in a small area outside his office. He popped corn twice a day, creating that distinctive and delicious smell that attracted others to the area.

Action Idea: Take the ocean liner approach. For introverts, building a common ground can take a long time. Give yourself the necessary time by reframing the process as an extended journey across the Atlantic, sailing on a majestic ocean liner. Realize that you have the entire journey to develop a common ground with certain people. View each day as another step in the process. You can create a link during a lunch break or while strolling through the workplace.

Provide Valued Resources

Quantum Leaders cultivate leader-quality relationships by providing others with valued resources. The operative word is *valued*. With an understanding that any resource's value is defined by the person who receives the resource, Quantum Leaders provide people with resources *they* want, not what the leader wants. Quantum Leaders also know that resources are more valuable when people cannot easily get them from other sources. Quantum Leaders gain distinction by providing scarce resources.

Identify Valued Resources

Quantum Leaders consciously pursue, ask about, listen for, and observe what matters to others. This may sound elementary, but it is not an elementary reality. In a June 1991 article in *Fortune,* Faye Rice cited a 1990 poll conducted by the management consulting company Towers Perrin, which showed fewer than half of the employees surveyed believing that management was aware of the problems they faced. Rice also reported that the Hay Group, another consulting organization, found that of more than 1 million employees from 2,000 organizations, only 34 percent said that their company listened to them well.

Action Idea: Conduct a valued resources needs analysis. Conduct a meeting where you ask people, "What resources do you value?" Give them a list of possible resources (e.g., wages, appreciation, promotion, being kept informed, job security, working conditions, understanding about personal problems) as a starting point, and ask them to add to the list. Then they rank the items from most to least important. There is no magic to this process. It is a nuts-and-bolts question-and-answer session. I recommend revisiting this analysis at least twice a year or after any significant event that affects the organization (e.g., a shift in competitive focus, organizational restructuring, a change of management).

Define the Resources You Control and Those You Do Not

No Quantum Leader controls the full range of resources people want from work. The increasing press for "lean and mean" companies has almost eliminated the promise of lifetime employment, and salary increases and promotions, which were never given nonchalantly, are even more competitive. Quantum Leaders take a proactive approach by defining the resources they can and cannot control.

> *Action Idea: Clarify what you can and cannot provide.* Clarify those resources you control and those you do not control. Then explain to employees the boundaries of your authority and the limits to your flexibility regarding resource acquisition and distribution. Focus on acquiring and providing the valued resources you do control.

> *Action Idea: Explain the system.* Tell people, to the best of your ability, how your organizational resource allocation system works. Explain the processes used to mete out wages, job security, working conditions, promotions, and softer resources such as information, access, and recognition. This discussion requires complete candor. Tell people what you know, clarify what you do not know about orga-

nizational systems, and seek ways to improve your knowledge about them.

Provide the Resources That You Do Control

If you control resources such as pay, promotion, working conditions, equipment, and vacation time, provide them when people deserve them. My experience with organizations reveals that people have a higher degree of control over soft resources, such as appreciation, recognition, access to information, challenging work opportunities, and involvement in decision making. More important, these resources are often highly valued. In their 1982 study, *In Search of Excellence,* Peters and Waterman found that excellent companies pay attention to appreciating, involving, and showing concern for their employees.

In my consulting work, employees regularly tell me that they do not feel their managers give them enough voice in what goes on in the company. They tell me they are "sure" their managers withhold information from them. Quantum Leaders do work to acquire the hard resources such as pay and promotion, but they also focus on providing the soft resources because they usually have greater control over them. Three soft resources seem especially important today: appreciation, visibility, and professional opportunity. Quantum Leaders have significant latitude to provide these resources.

Appreciation

Perhaps the most valued resource you can provide to others is to make them feel valued by appreciating them. People move in the direction where they are appreciated. Appreciation transforms interpersonal relationships, because when people appreciate us, they tune into our particular awareness frequency, defined as MMFG-AM (Make Me Feel Good About Myself). Everyone wants to feel good about themselves, and appreciation helps people possess that feeling. Quantum Leaders tune into each person's specific wavelength of MMFG-AM.

Appreciation and the desire to experience MMFG-AM are imprinted early in childhood. Adults often notice babies. They make funny faces and gurgle sounds to get the baby's attention, they coo soft words and wave or wiggle their hands at the baby, and they smile at the baby to try to make the infant smile back. Babies are showered with positive stimuli from all the people around them. If the baby cries or appears uncomfortable, a gaggle of helpful people gather to offer suggestions and counsel on how to soothe the baby. When a baby is hungry, or has a wet diaper, or is hurt, most people, even complete strangers, move quickly to remedy the situation and to help the baby feel better. These experiences create a significant impression in the baby's consciousness. The continuous stream of messages from the environment says to the baby: "You matter to us," "We care about your welfare," and "We want to make you feel good."

As we grow older, our favored-person status begins to disappear, and people stop taking notice of us. When we are tired, fearful, or hurt, few people take time to even recognize our discomfort, much less do something to make us feel better. Yet the memory of MMFG-AM remains within our awareness. When we meet someone who helps us feel good, an instant connection occurs. The appreciation regenerates that sense of unconditional self-worth we experienced as infants.

> *Action Idea: Tune In to MMFG-AM.* Spend 10 minutes each day focusing on ways to appreciate people. Praise some aspect of their work you find admirable. Recognize their contribution at a meeting. Tell people you are glad to be working with them when the circumstance warrants it.

> *Action Idea: Thank people.* Say thank you, and say it often when people do even the slightest thing for you. Basic, right? Yet thanking people is a discipline that few people truly master. It requires practice and focused attention.

> *Action Idea: Create an "applause newsletter."* An "applause newsletter" recounts people's work contributions,

both major and mundane. Write the first five issues of the newsletter yourself.

Action Idea: Hold success celebrations. On a regular basis, formally celebrate the successes of your people. As reported in a 1992 *Fortune* magazine article, every Saturday, top executives at Wal-Mart get together to review the week's activities. Chief Operating Officer Don Soderquist reads the honor roll of stores that showed the greatest improvement over the corresponding week a year ago.

Action Idea: Create a "company hero" program. Designate an informal reward, "The Company Hero," to be given when someone goes above and beyond the call of duty in even a modest way. Create a certificate to symbolize the award, and present it with the proper ceremony of gratitude.

Action Idea: Send "I heard something good about you" notes. When you hear of someone's accomplishments from others, send the person an "I Heard Something Good About You" note. Write 10 notes each month.

Visibility and Professional Opportunity

Two other valued resources Quantum Leaders can fairly easily provide to cultivate leader-quality relationships are visibility and professional opportunity, which reinforce each other. Visibility meets our need to be noticed and to feel important. It helps us be a part of what is going on. Professional opportunity offers us access to arenas for achievement where we can demonstrate our skills and experience. It allows us the chance to grow and develop.

Action Idea: Send people with their report. Sending people with their report provides an avenue for both visibility and professional opportunity. Consider what typically happens when a person pours tremendous amounts of time and energy into developing a truly excellent report, which then is presented by someone else. The presenter receives an intense wave of appreciation for the effort; the report preparer gets only a secondhand accounting of the positive reaction. Sending people with their report makes them visible to get the firsthand approval response to the report and provides a platform for them to demonstrate their professional expertise. This action idea will not work for someone who does not like to speak in front of a group, and in some situations it is not possible or appropriate.

Action Idea: Include people at a meeting. Allow people to attend a meeting with you that they would like to attend but normally do not. Access to the meeting provides an opportunity to demonstrate their expertise or make a contribution.

Action Idea: Help a "10-yarder" across the goal line. A "10-yarder" is someone who is close to succeeding on an important task. He or she will succeed eventually, but your help can provide a boost. A manager from a large company knew that a staff assistant in his division wanted a transfer to a position that had more challenge and responsibility. She would have gotten the new assignment eventually, but the manager placed a telephone call to support the assistant's application. His action sped up the process to have the position offered to this assistant. The manager's effort pushed her request along to expedite the process and helped her score.

Develop Trust

Trust binds people together in leader-quality relationships. Common ground requires a solid confidence that the person is trustworthy. Common ground crumbles when suspicion infects the relationship. The impact of valued resources depends on the beliefs people have about your intentions. Efforts to appreciate others or to provide them with other important resources lose their impact when people suspect your motives. People will hide their interests and will not reveal the resources they value to a person they mistrust.

Trust is a quantum phenomenon because it unites us in a seamless field of interdependence. Distrust drives people apart; it reinforces the classical physics sense of separateness. We do not give unqualified trust to someone who is not and cannot be a part of us; rather, we operate with wariness, destructive competitiveness, and even harsh aggressiveness. We trust people who are like us, and we do not trust people who are dissimilar to us. Sadly, the importance of trust still eludes some organizations.

Quantum Leaders know that trust begets trust. When they trust people, Quantum Leaders encourage people's involvement and they show confidence in others, who are galvanized to show more initiative and greater allegiance. People respond with more openness. Positive results occur, and people feel a sense of pride. The Quantum Leader's trust is confirmed. In contrast, when someone distrusts another, he or she tends to overly control and doubt the person. The person responds with apathy, resentment, and hesitancy. Efforts falter, and the person neglects work and operates with secrecy. Distrust is confirmed.

Jack Stack, CEO of Springfield Remanufacturing Corporation (SRC) in Springfield, Missouri, turned SRC around from a losing venture in 1983 to a debt-free, $77 million-a-year company by 1992 by establishing a climate of trust. At SRC, all employees, even line workers, are trained to understand company financial statements—income statements, balance sheets, cash flow statements, and so forth. They help develop standard accounting costs, compute variances for their own work, calculate and interpret financial indicators and financial ratios, and understand how the company's stock is evaluated and how their work affects stock values. Stack's openness demonstrates his trust in others, and that translates into bottom-line results.

Trust building begins within the Quantum Leader's intention to be trustworthy and to trust others.*

> *Action Idea: Tell the truth.* This one sounds like a no-brainer, but the most important ingredient in building trust is telling the truth. Trust and truth telling go hand in hand. Telling the truth is also easier, because it is easy to remember the truth while it may take some thought to remember a lie. I tell business and government executives that they will usually get caught when they lie. Most people are not very good actors, and they give themselves away when they lie. Do not equivocate. Tell the truth.

> *Action Idea: Make and follow through on 10 commitments.* Make 10 observable promises and keep them. People learn not to trust those who do not do what they say they will do.

> *Action Idea: Trust others first.* A red flag goes up when you ask people to trust you as a condition for your trusting them. Offer your trust first, as a way to gain the trust of others.

> *Action Idea: Extend your trust of others.* If you already display trust, extend that display with greater trust. Increase the latitude you provide to people. Trusting others more makes you more trustworthy in their eyes.

> *Action Idea: Protect core interests.* Protect what matters most to people. We trust those who look out for our core interests.

> *Action Idea: Eliminate secret meetings.* Secret meetings send a message that you do not trust people. Abolish them.

*Several of the following action ideas are based on ideas in *Managing Transitions,* by William Bridges.

Action Idea: Use your three I's. Your three I's are involve, inform, and include. Involvement in decision making gives people a sense of ownership. Involve people in discussions about important issues. Information is power. Inform people of what is going on. Inclusion creates a sense of belonging. Include people in decision making. Your three I's show people you trust them with power.

Action Idea: Get your but *out of your conversation.* When we use *but* in our conversations, we negate what was just said. For example, consider these statements: "You did a good job, *but* I have some suggestions." "I enjoyed this time together, *but* I have a meeting to go to now." The word *but* negates the previous part of each statement. Mixed messages limit trust. Take the word *but* out of your language as much as possible, and replace it with *and*. For example, "You did a good job, *and* I have some suggestions." "I enjoyed this time together, *and* I have a meeting to go to now." The word *and* changes the meaning. It sends a congruent message.

Action Idea: Give trust building time. Trust building takes time. People are cautious as a form of self-protection, and they do not give up self-protection easily. Give your trust-building efforts time to germinate. With consistent application of the action ideas suggested in this chapter, trust will pervade your relationships.

Build Credibility

Credibility represents the unified point value of leader-quality relationships. Like DNA, credibility contains the entire coding structure of a relationship. Common ground, valued resources, and trust converge into the focal point of leader-quality relationships known as credibility. When a person is credible, others believe in that person and perceive the person as dependable, reliable, and worthy of support.

Invisible Points

Credibility can be viewed as invisible points that people ascribe to a leader. The more points or credits a leader has, the greater is the leader's credibility. Everything a leader does affects the point total. People give points when common ground gets established, valued resources are provided, and trust is demonstrated. They give points to the leader who matches values, effectively reframes events, speaks in the codes of the follower's private mental language, and maps the territory and charts a course that meets the follower's needs. People take points away when the leader fails to do these things.

With enough credits or points, the possibilities to gain and maintain the confidence of others increase. A very high degree of credibility provides the leader with tremendous influence. Consider the frightening reality that Jim Jones's credibility was so high at the time of the Guyana tragedy in 1976 that he could convince 900 men and women to kill their children and then commit mass suicide. When credibility is destroyed, little can be done to maintain support. Despite the landslide presidential victories of Lyndon Johnson in 1964, Richard Nixon in 1972, and George Bush in 1988, each of their political careers ended soon afterward because they lost so many credits. In contrast, leaders with enough points can maintain support even after they lose significant credibility. Remember that Ronald Reagan's response to the Iran-contra affair in 1986 was, "I don't remember." Reagan's credits declined because of this statement, but he had so much credibility that voters accepted his memory lapse.

Quantum Leaders know that credits are governed by the follower's subjective consciousness: What might be credible to one person may not signify credibility to another. Additionally, potential followers require varying degrees of credits before they accept the leader as credible. Some people demand a large number of credits; others require only a few. Until the Quantum

Leader passes the necessary credit threshold, the leader does not have the necessary credibility.

Frank, a manager in a wholesale and retail products company, gained credibility very quickly with the company president because Frank had effective customer service skills. It took him much longer to establish the necessary credits with the vice president of operations. Frank finally passed the critical threshold with the operations vice president when he started coming to work early, staying late, and taking on extra projects, which were the operations vice president's key credibility indicators.

Credits can amass slowly over time—but they can be lost in a moment. Gary Hart's 1988 bid for the Democratic presidential nomination seemed almost certain based on his previous political record and his successful showing in the early days of the race. But Hart's credibility was stripped almost overnight because of an indiscretion.

Building Credibility

Quantum Leaders intentionally seek ways to build their credibility to help cultivate leader-quality relationships.

> *Action Idea: Find out what people perceive as credible.* Ask people what they feel indicates credibility. Have them define the specific behaviors that demonstrate credibility.

> *Action Idea: Demonstrate your credibility.* If people in your organization tell you that work-related expertise demonstrates credibility, develop expertise and then actively seek ways to display it. If credibility means helping others, do so. This action idea does not mean being underhanded or manipulative. Quantum Leaders always refer back to their intention when implementing an action such as this. They use this action idea with the sincere intention of cultivating leader-quality relationships that benefit others. We have total control over our intention at all times.

Action Idea: Admit mistakes. Integrity increases credibility. The rash of cover-ups, fraud, and underhanded dealings in government and industry has jaded many people, and cynicism runs rampant today. In a poll reported on June 8, 1985, in the *New York Times,* only 32 percent of the public indicated they believe most corporate executives are honest, with 55 percent saying they think executives are dishonest. This survey was done *before* the massive nationwide savings and loan crisis victimized over 350 institutions and produced 331 convictions of "respectable bankers." Admitting mistakes distinguishes you from the unsavory lot who try to conceal their mistakes.

Leader-Quality Relationships in Perspective

Relationship building is like sex: Almost everyone believes they understand the importance of it, almost everyone thinks it involves performing some "natural ability," and, most important, almost everyone thinks that relationship problems are caused by the other person. Quantum Leaders know that they hold the responsibility—the ability to respond—to the quality of relationships they develop.

No person can ever cultivate the requisite quality of relationship needed to win over all people. *The seventh natural law of leadership* explains that not everyone will follow your lead. Quantum Leaders keep their relationship-building activity in perspective, focusing on critical relationships. The field of relationships cannot be controlled in a dictatorial fashion, so Quantum Leaders nurture relationships as a gardener cares for a garden: by planting seeds, tending them as they grow, and accepting when some do not sprout.

12

Quantum Leaders vs. Classical Managers

"The leader leads, and the boss drives."

—*Theodore Roosevelt*

What are the differences between a leader and a manager? This question plagues countless people I meet. Managers want to be leaders, but they are unclear about what that means. Training directors want to develop leaders within their organization, but they cannot clearly define what has to be done to develop the skills or behaviors that identify leaders. And personnel directors want to recruit leaders for their organizations, but they have no framework by which to measure potential leaders.

Quantum Leadership explicitly reveals that a manager is not necessarily a leader. The common research approach of discussing "leadership" findings based on an analysis of managers is inappropriate. The media also misdirect us when they label as leaders those who hold the title of manager, a position in government, or head of a club, company, or country.

The Fundamental Distinctions

The natural laws of leadership and the Quantum Leadership paradigm provides a clear distinction between leaders and managers: Leaders are better understood as a quantum phenomenon, while managers are well described through the classical physics lens. Quantum Leaders differ from classical managers in five ways:

Classical Managers	Quantum Leaders
1. Have subordinates	1. Attract willing followers
2. Use influence based on formal authority	2. Develop influence beyond authority
3. Operate within prescribed pathways	3. Operate outside prescribed pathways
4. Are given a position	4. Take initiative to lead
5. Rely on tradition and procedure	5. Rely on consciousness

Subordinates vs. Followers

The first natural law of leadership provides the fundamental distinction between managers and leaders: Managers have subordinates who are defined as separate entities by by the permanent lines of authority described in an organizational chart; Quantum Leaders attract willing followers to create a field of interaction, a relationship *(the second natural law)*. The manager and subordinate roles exist as a continuous reality defined by position. Specific people who occupy those roles may change, but the roles are an ongoing reality of the organization. Quantum Leadership is discontinuous *(the third natural law)* because the field of interaction manifests when leaders attract followers.

Formal Authority vs. Influence Beyond Authority

Managers rely on influence based on formal authority. Using deterministic, predictable rules, regulations, policies, and procedures as the basis of their power, they apply the classical physics concepts of force and pressure to control people's behavior. The manager, operating from a "superior" position as "the boss," a separate entity from subordinates, commands subordinates to comply with the authority given by the organization.

Influence in the Quantum Leadership field stems from the interaction between leader and follower *(the fourth natural law of leadership)*. Quantum Leaders bond and unite with followers as allies, and that unity generates the power of leadership. Quantum Leaders start where the followers are, connect with them, and then lead them where the Quantum Leader wants to go.

An organizational chart spells out the prescribed lines of formal authority and maps the deterministic reporting relationships between managers and subordinates. With a classical physics mind-set, people rely on the chart to answer the question, "Where do I fit in?" The field of Quantum Leadership interaction is better described as a web of relationships, an intricate network of connections. The central node of the web represents the Quantum Leader in any given leadership event. Threads that bond the Quantum Leader to the followers spread out in an array of linkages, some more directly connected than others (Figure 12-1).

Figure 12-1. Classical-manager vs. Quantum-Leader authority.

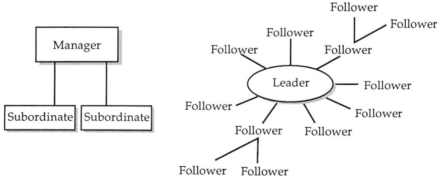

Prescribed Pathways vs. Doing More Than Is Prescribed

Classical managers implement prescribed rules, regulations, policies, and procedures. They see that orders are carried out, and they control people and systems to ensure assigned duties are completed. Management theory focuses on orderliness, structure, and stability.

Established procedures do not apply *(the fifth natural law of leadership)* in the arena where Quantum Leaders operate. Quantum Leaders do more than is prescribed. They operate in the uncertain leadership arena that exists outside the boundaries of organization rules and regulation. Quantum Leadership clarifies the need for awareness of uncertainty.

Both managers and leaders do the right things, and they both do things right. Managers deserve credit when they effectively complete established missions along defined pathways. Quantum Leaders deserve recognition because they emerge when the existing pathway fails to provide direction. They operate in the uncertain, probabilistic, changing realm where organizational policies do not apply and people do not know what to do *(the sixth natural law of leadership)*. Managers receive organizational recognition when they get people to do what they are supposed to do. Quantum Leaders gain credibility by guiding followers to take unique action that overcomes nonprescribed problems and exploit opportunities.

Given a Role vs. Taking Initiative

Managers are given a role and asked to fulfill the requirements defined by its prescribed authority, responsibility, and accountability. Subordinates are obligated to comply with the manager's demands. Quantum Leaders take the risk of initiative to resolve uncertainty *(the sixth natural law of leadership)*. They do not always get the commitment they seek from others *(the seventh natural law of leadership)*.

Tradition and Procedure vs. Consciousness

Classical managers rely on tradition and procedure to get things done. They go by the book to determine direction, and they demand compliance from others. Quantum Leadership is based on consciousness—the capacity to process information. By using their consciousness to map the territory and chart a course, Quantum Leaders create a connection of consciousness to gain committed followers. The Quantum Leadership field exists as a shared wave of information-energy.

Two in One: The Manager as Quantum Leader

I do not mean to imply a value judgment that leaders are better than managers. The recent surge of manager bashing, which denigrates the managerial role as a second-class occupation, reveals flawed thinking about the differences between managers and leaders. We need both managers and Quantum Leaders to steer people and organizations forward.

Anyone selected or promoted to a managerial position deserves credit for being recognized as qualified to fulfill the managerial requirement. Managers also deserve encouragement to carry out the difficult duties associated with meeting prescribed deadlines, motivating others to complete assigned duties, and ensuring that results meet defined goals. In today's challenging times, managers face even greater demands than in the past.

The most productive managers are those who also take the lead to resolve the uncertainty inherent in the leadership arena. Such managers merit even greater recognition. People typically expect managers to function as leaders. People usually look to the person in charge when they need direction within the confines of prescribed rules and especially within the unpredictability of the leadership arena. This reality provides an advantage for managers who seek to lead.

Quantum Leadership is not a better role than management, just as quantum physics is not better or more real than classical physics. Both are valid in their respective domains. The laws of nature that govern quantum physics and Quantum Leadership differ from those that regulate classical physics and management. When you require someone to do something because of prescribed rules, you contend with classical physics. When you want to move your consciousness and the consciousness of others to take initiative in the leadership arena, you experience the quantum reality of leadership.

Some people have bifocal consciousness: the capacity to process information as a classical physics manager and as a Quantum Leader. They hold others accountable and enforce their compliance to fulfill the managerial requirement, and they are willing to take the risks associated with venturing beyond the boundaries of established procedures and gaining willing followers.

David Bell, director of the Management Services Division within the Department of Agriculture, models such behavior. When he took over the director's position, he held an off-site workshop for branch chiefs where they generated ideas about how the division could be more productive and could respond to change and uncertainty. Under Bell's guidance, the group made several important decisions about how to realign the organization for the future. The branch chiefs were enthusiastic about their new ability to participate and eagerly followed Bell's lead. Yet Bell also put on his managerial hat when one of his staff members failed to follow through on several directives regarding implementation of the off-site meetings initiatives. No amount of leader influence had any impact, so Bell resorted to his managerial authority by defining the staff member's responsibility and accountability for results.

Bell confided to me that in some respects it was more difficult functioning as a manager. He found leading the branch chiefs stimulating. In contrast, using managerial force to overcome the staff member's resistance was gut wrenching and draining.

Not all managers operate with bifocal consciousness. Rather, they rely almost completely on the power of their managerial position. "Kick butt and take names" is a phrase I still hear throughout the ranks of managers in business and government. For example, a manager of a chemical plant I know works from 6:00 A.M. to 7:00 P.M. five days a week, and he comes to the plant on his days off "just to see how things are going." I admire Jerry's dedication and willingness to work hard, but I also recognize his tendency to overcontrol. Jerry relies on the phrase "Because I told you to," when directing others. He regularly reminds people, "It's my responsibility to make sure you do it right."

Jerry is locked into the mind-set that visible authority gets results. He sets himself apart from others, and he attempts to ensure outcomes through the force of his constant physical presence at the plant and his dominant will. Jerry drives himself and others in an effort that he believes will determine with great certainty the outcomes of the unit. He believes, "If I spend enough time and if I pressure the system enough, things will work out."

Jerry gets the job done. When situations are "in order," the unit runs smoothly. If obstacles arise and people and processes get stuck in unforeseen ruts, which happens often because of unexpected change and uncertainty, Jerry expedites. He works harder and pushes people. He gets results, but he exhausts himself through reliance on force, and he wears others down through constant pressure. He operates within a limited mind-set and does not take advantage of all the laws of nature that govern human interaction.

Quantum Leader Effectiveness

All managers and all leaders want to be effective. Managerial effectiveness can be determined by how well the manager carries out prescribed rules, regulations, policies, and procedures. Effective managers meet established requirements, gain compliance from others, and achieve stated objectives.

Effective Quantum Leadership cannot be measured in this way because its arena transcends these standards. Quantum Leadership occurs in arenas of uncertainty, and it requires gaining subjective commitment of followers-allies, not enforcing the objective manager-subordinate line of authority. Thus, "effective" leadership is subjective; it depends on the viewpoint of the observer. When we evaluate leaders, we are all residents of

Missouri, the "show me" state. Leaders and their methods are assessed differently by different people based on what the leader demonstrates and represents to the followers. As a way to understand leadership effectiveness, I categorize leaders as "the good, the bad, and the ugly."

Good Leaders

Think of someone you have willingly followed who helped you to achieve a goal. That person represents a good leader to you. Americans who supported George Bush in Operation Desert Storm believed the war just, and they were glad the Iraqi forces were defeated. For them, Bush was a good leader in this situation. Those who willingly supported Jack Welch at GE during the massive employment cuts and organizational restructuring and who believed these changes benefited the company consider Welch a good leader. A "good" leader is someone you follow who helps you to achieve a goal.

Bad Leaders

Have you ever followed someone and the result was failure— that is, you did not accomplish what you had hoped? For you, that person is a bad leader. You followed, but the leader did not take you where you wanted to go.

In the late 1980s, James Robinson III, CEO at American Express, projected a bold vision for the company: to transform it into a global financial empire. Robinson had the support of many, but according to *Business Week*, Robinson's vision failed. In 1993, he was ousted by the company's board of directors.

Bad leaders are also defined as those who take followers in the direction the leader initially charted; however, when the followers get there, they realize it is not the place they want to be. Consider George Bush again. The majority of Americans supported him in 1988 on a presidential platform that essentially argued America needed to stay the course. Voters agreed with Bush that no major domestic crises faced America, so Bush focused his efforts on international affairs. By 1992, staying the course appeared to be a mistake: Americans felt their president needed to focus attention on domestic issues. In 1992, Bush was seen as a "bad" leader. He had led his followers in the direction they initially supported, but they did not want to be where he had taken them.

Ugly Leaders

To understand the ugly leader, think of someone *you* will not follow, but whom others do follow. For example, few Americans today would admit to being willing followers of Saddam Hussein. During World War II, Americans did not support Adolph Hitler. For Americans, Hussein and Hitler are the ugly leaders. Of course, Hussein and Hitler possess or did possess huge numbers of followers, so what is ugly to one person is good to another.

Ineffective Leaders

Leadership effectiveness is subjective—a quantum phenomenon. Leaders can be good, bad, or ugly depending on how people look at them. The continual quest to define effective leaders explores barren territory until we accept the quantum reality of leadership.

It might simply be that the term *ineffective leader* is a misnomer, or perhaps we need to define leadership ineffectiveness as a failed attempt to gain followers. Ineffective leadership could also be defined as a situation in which no leader emerges and a leadership vacuum exists. That is, when people hope, expect, and need direction but they get nothing, problems remain or opportunities pass. No one takes the risk of initiative to lead, so no one has a chance to follow.

Are You a Quantum Leader or a Classical Physics Manager?

To answer this question, consider why people do what you ask. Is their behavior performed as compliance with your formal authority? Are you directing them to comply with the prescribed path of their job and to fulfill the organization's established strategy, goals, and plans? If you answer yes to these questions, then you are a manager. Good! We need effective managers who get others to do what they are supposed to do and who fulfill their organization's stated mission.

Now also consider: Are people willingly following your direction? Is your influence based on commitment to you, the person, regardless of your position? Are you directing others to go beyond the boundaries, to join you in the risk of taking advantage of an unknown opportunity or of finding a way to overcome an obstacle? If you answer yes to these questions, you are in the Quantum Leadership arena.

13

Developing the Quantum Leader Within

"Before we start talking, let's decide what we are talking about."

—Socrates

Can leaders be developed? Or are some people "natural-born" leaders? Fundamentally, Quantum Leadership development encompasses the development of consciousness. Quantum Leadership can be developed by expanding consciousness.

Quantum Leadership Development as Consciousness Expansion

Quantum Leadership development involves expanding consciousness in terms of the "three C's": chemistry, character, and culture.

Chemistry, our neurophysiological processes, defines the *capacity to be conscious*. To use a computer metaphor, our mind-body chemistry, its neural and structural faculties, represents the human hardware of consciousness. Quantum Leadership development requires that we restructure the human hardware.

Consciousness expansion begins by upgrading the human bio-computer.

Character, our information-processing methods, defines the *ability to apply consciousness*. The mind-set we use to perceive represents the human software of consciousness. Quantum Leadership development requires new or reprogrammed versions of our quantum sense: the capacity to perceive what others don't; the ability to go into the G.A.P. and transcend the conditioned response to knee-jerk thinking; the skill at performing enlightened action to create shared meaning.

Culture, the collective mind-set and organizationally structured methods of interaction, affects the flow and display of consciousness. Group norms and organizational systems represent the *network of consciousness*. Quantum Leadership development requires alterations in organizational systems so that both leaders and followers are rewarded as cocreators of leadership power.

This threefold approach of developing chemistry, character, and culture, or hardware, software, and network, offers a solid foundation to develop Quantum Leadership.

Upgrading the Human Hardware

The human hardware, the brain and nervous system, represents the circuitry of consciousness. When the mind-body operates properly, we function with an active, focused awareness while feeling stable and relaxed. In contrast, when the human hardware breaks down, consciousness cannot flow effectively. We experience the breakdown as feeling dull, fatigued, and inflexible. Our capacity to pay attention is restricted. Discrimination becomes cloudy. Initiative wanes. Performance suffers. We react by trying harder, which exacerbates the problem by straining a fragile system. The impact on consciousness of a stable circuitry and an effectively functioning biochemistry is typically unnoticed until the system breaks down. Burnout is usually viewed as a psychological malady, yet the lack of energy, motivation, and concentration symptomatic of burnout is associated with dramatic changes in blood pressure and other biochemical changes.

Quantum Leadership development begins with a comprehensive fitness program, which improves the circuitry and biochemistry that form the capacity to be conscious. Today fitness programs are recognized as important to performance, yet to expand consciousness, a workout program needs to go beyond simply toning up or slimming down. Continual maintenance and improvement of the human biocomputer circuitry is needed through a mind-body fitness program.

An integrated program of diet, exercise, and behavior management can upgrade the human hardware. Whatever methods one uses must suit the needs, interests, and desires of the practitioner. To upgrade the human hardware by improving some very fundamental habits for eating, exercise, rest, and life-style requires finding a routine that fits where you are now. I suggest going into the G.A.P. to explore the utility of any mind-body program that has been shown to develop consciousness.

> *Action Idea: Investigate mind-body fitness regimens.* Talk to friends. Review the appropriate literature (look for references to consciousness, mind-body medicine, or executive health in books and magazines). Ask your doctor. Review the alternatives to find something that appeals to you.

> *Action Idea: Begin a program within 30 days.* Knowing how to upgrade mind-body capacities becomes useful only by doing something. Translate your research into a specific action plan. Then start it right away.

> *Action Idea: Avoid the "no pain–no gain" approach to exercise.* The "no pain–no gain" approach assumes that you have to push yourself to your limit and then let the system recover. Recent mind-body fitness innovations, however, suggest this approach may be antithetical to overall biochemical adaptability and stability. Dr. John Douillard recommends a more enlightened approach to exercise in his

book *Body, Mind and Sport.* He suggests that exercise should rejuvenate mind-body effectiveness, not reduce its energy, and that a workout should remove stress, not create it. Mind-body fitness should improve mind-body coordination, not break it down.

Action Idea: Learn a meditation technique. Because of the voluminous scientific research supporting the beneficial impact of meditation, it appears essential to include some form of meditation in your mind-body fitness program. Research on Transcendental Meditation (TM) shows it has a positive impact on neurophysiological functioning.

Reprogramming the Human Software

Our mind-set establishes the perceptual framework through which we receive, interpret, and respond to information. The approach we take to map the territory and chart a course, our skill at going into the G.A.P. and perceiving what others don't, and the flexibility to reframe and match the follower's internal information processing codes are all structured within our personal paradigm.

Action Idea: Review previous action ideas. The action ideas provided in Chapters 5 through 7 specifically focus on ways to reprogram the software of consciousness. Review those action ideas as part of your program for consciousness expansion.

Restructuring the Group Consciousness Network

Individual leadership development is reinforced when leaders are developed throughout an organization. The network of group consciousness, an organization's culture, provides a platform to enhance leadership, but it can also create constraints on leadership. Quantum Leaders can shape organizational change but must also reflect collective consciousness. The leader cannot be too far ahead of the pack, or few followers will have any idea where the leader is. To develop Quantum Leaders means creating an organizational culture that develops consciousness in everyone.

Several steps can be taken to restructure the group consciousness network. Because of their scope, these steps will have to be taken by those at the top of the organization or those who can gain followers from senior levels.

Action Idea: Institute mind-body fitness programs. Set up in-house programs that provide mind-body fitness knowledge and techniques. Corporate wellness programs or companies that provide stress management training are a step in this direction.

Action Idea: Reward both leaders and followers. Reinforce individuals who take the risk of initiative, perceive from the G.A.P., and develop influence beyond authority. And recognize and reward followers as vital contributors to the Quantum Leadership field. Such efforts change the organizational culture from one that rewards only managerial activity to one that rewards leadership action.

Action Idea: Redirect the "boo rulers." Those who process information as negative doubters, destructive critics, and hopeless cynics restrict the flow of collective consciousness. Quantum Leaders challenge and question but do not limit information flow with incessant booing. Redirect the information processing assassins who negate Quantum Leadership practices when they use phrases such as, "We've done okay without it," "I do this now anyway," and "It's a gimmick, a fad, a trick." Institutionalize behaviors that are proactive, positive, and progressive. Change the organization's reward system so that "boo rulers" are not positively reinforced.

Action Idea: Recognize the restrictive culture roots. Organizations with destructive information processing cultures can be recognized by various roots: the tendency to let information sort itself out rather than sorting it out themselves; the practice of waiting until pressures from any source define what to do rather than proactively deciding what to do; the reliance on outside experts and waiting to be told rather than on individual instincts and being proactive; a lack of cooperation and trust; a failure to reward innovation; and a lack of support for new ideas. If these culture roots exist, consciously label them as outdated. Identify behaviors that reinforce the negative roots, and change those behaviors with skill training and facilitation.

Initiate a Quantum Leader Consciousness Development Plan

When Do You Begin? Now!

While playing for the New York Mets, Tom Seaver once asked Yogi Berra, "Hey, Yogi, what time is it?" Berra responded, "You mean now?" Quantum Leadership development begins *now*. And it begins again the next time you realize it is now. The process never ends.

> *Action Idea: Establish a continuous consciousness improvement plan.* "When you are green you're growing. When you're ripe, you rot," said Ray Kroc, founder of MacDonald's. Stay green. Initiate a lifelong learning plan, and then stick to it with regular and dedicated practice. Do not ride the waves of change; make the waves.

How Do You Begin? A Workout Plan

To develop your Quantum Leadership capacity, establish a workout plan.

Action Idea: Define your goals. What aspect of Quantum Leadership do you want to master? Improved neurophysiological functioning? The ability to go effortlessly into the G.A.P.? The capacity to recognize and match the internal codes of private mental language? Write your goals on paper in clear, specific, measurable language.

Action Idea: Use "the perfect practice makes perfect" approach. The widespread belief that "practice makes perfect" is incorrect. Some people have years of practice doing things wrong. Using the "perfect practice makes perfect" approach means applying a skill based on the well-designed mechanics behind it. Quantum Leadership development requires practice with guidance. Whatever direction you choose to improve yourself, continually refer back to the mechanics that describe the process. Effective Quantum Leadership practice requires artful implementation based on an application of the mechanics that guide that art.

Action Idea: Break through the blocks of the past. Think back to an action plan for any task that you did not follow through to completion. Identify the causes for your lack of completion. Then set up the conditions to break through these causes. For example, perhaps you did not follow through because you did not allow adequate time. Get past this block by scheduling time on your calendar for your Quantum Leadership consciousness development workout.

Action Idea: Anticipate feeling awkward. Altering your diet or life-style regime or implementing a new set of behaviors can be difficult. When we do something new or unfamiliar, we can become frustrated by the intense effort and lack of comfort we feel. The awkwardness created by personal change efforts can throw us off course. Anticipate this awkwardness, and prepare yourself so that you are ready to overcome it. Reframe the experience before it happens. Acknowledge that everyone feels this way sometimes. Feel good about the fact that you recognize the awkwardness for what it is—a part of the developmental process.

Action Idea: Avoid using external standards to measure your progress. To keep on track, compare your progress only with yourself. It might take a peer only a few weeks to master reframing, while your progress might be slower. If you use this peer as your standard, you can become discouraged. Remember the subjective nature of quantum life. Develop an inner standard to determine your progress. Compare where you are to where you were, not to someone else.

Action Idea: Vary your workout. Practice applying your skills in different situations with different people. Being able to focus your attention into the G.A.P. on the shop floor does not necessarily translate into doing so in a meeting with senior management or critical customers.

Action Idea: Create a support system. It is much easier to meditate or get to the gym every day if you have other people to do it with you. It will be easier to stay on your Quantum Leadership consciousness development workout if you involve others. Ask people to join your effort. A support system has the bonus of developing the leadership capacity of others within your organization.

Action Idea: Use your mistakes as learning opportunities. Mistakes do not become problems unless you refuse to accept them for what they are: learning events. An old adage is that success comes from good work, good work is the result of experience, and experience is often the result of doing poor work. By definition, the leadership arena involves risk and uncertainty, which means you will not always do the right thing. Use your mistakes to redirect your thinking and action so that you continually do better.

The Invisible University

"Wisdom is not the product of schooling but of the life-long attempt to acquire it," said Albert Einstein. Any arena can be a learning event to develop Quantum Leader consciousness if you enroll in what Ron Gross, in his book *Peak Learning*, calls the Invisible University: the set of classrooms and instructors made up of everyday life experiences. Students in the Invisible University can learn from any source, at any time, in any place. The motto of this all-inclusive institution is, "Bloom where you are planted." Taking an Invisible University class means you define your leadership learning goal, select the teachers and classroom where you want to learn, and set out to master the lesson.

For example, if you want to expand your consciousness about performing enlightened action to influence others beyond authority, you might study the art of advertising and how the skilled craftspeople in this field persuade people to purchase products. You do not have to enroll in a marketing class at your local college or university, although that is one option; rather, you can create an Invisible University study program in your office or living room. Analyze the ads in magazines. Videotape television ads and analyze how the director gets the meaning of the message across. Ask others to give you their impressions of specific ads to understand how ads affect people differently. The point of the Invisible University is to make every day a learning day and to create as many learning events as you want without the constraints of formal, institutional boundaries.

Match your learning experiences to your information processing styles. If you are a visual person, you may gain insights by watching films that illustrate different elements of leadership practice. If you are an auditory type, cassette programs can be an important learning source. Producers of audiocassette programs have created tapes that fit the modern life-style. Because the average car ride is 20 minutes, most cassettes are packaged with complete 20-minute segments on each side. You can take an Invisible University course as part of your daily commuting activities.

Kinesthetic types, who learn best by feeling and action, might benefit from an outdoor challenge experience such as a ropes course or Outward Bound. For those who learn best by reading, the bookstore and library become an Invisible University feeding ground of food for thought. What books are worth reading, and which one should you read first? One way to decide is to select any book that has a title you find appealing. Skim its Table of Contents. Flip through the pages. Read a few passages. If you read something that you believe is important and you do not absolutely own that knowledge in theory or in practice, read that book. Study it. Do not get a second book until you master the content of the first.

The Hope for the Future

Can we develop the type of people to lead organizations to greater prosperity, to lead others to greater happiness and fulfillment, and to lead themselves with more inner contentment? The development of consciousness holds the key to foster more and better leadership. The difference between human DNA and gorilla DNA is said to be only 10 percent. A small percentage of development in consciousness can yield quantum leaps forward in the quality of leadership power in organizations.

You have the capacity to create that leap by contacting and developing the leader within you. Your consciousness is the source of Quantum Leader power in your organization. This power does not rely on any charter, vision statement, or constitution. This power is not a position someone holds. You have complete access to your consciousness. Goethe said, "Whatever you can do or dream, you can become it." You are the Quantum Leader. You own your consciousness, which makes you a custodian of leadership power. If you do not take lead, who will?

Each of us has a choice: to take the lead, even though we may not always gain followers and we may not achieve our goals, or languish in the background, unwilling to step forward and map the territory, hesitant to chart a course. Goethe also said, "Unless one is committed, there is hesitancy."

The Japanese believe that samurai warriors are as solid as the earth and as fluid as the water. The fully awakened leader within operates like a samurai. Quantum Leaders have a solid intention to lead. They focus their full attention on mapping the territory and charting a course they believe will resolve problems and exploit opportunities. Quantum Leaders also have the fluid adaptability of water. They meet the followers at the followers' level of consciousness. They use their discrimination to try alternate interpretations and to experiment with various routes.

Perfection is a moving target. Quantum Leaders' initiative is adaptable and generative because their consciousness is always moving. They take initiative with a full understanding of the natural law of successful action: If you do not get the result you want with one course of action, try something different.

Bibliography

The American Reader, ed. Diane Ravitch. New York: HarperCollins, 1990.

Bandler, Richard, and John Grinder. *Reframing,* eds. Steve Andreas and Connirae Andreas. Moab, Utah: Real People Press, 1982.

———. *Frogs Into Princes,* Moab, Utah: Real People Press, 1979.

Bechloss, Michael. *The Crisis Years.* New York: Harper-Collins, 1991, pp. 527–528. The idea of ignoring the second letter has been attributed to Robert F. Kennedy in most texts. Bechloss clarifies that it was Bundy's idea and that Bundy graciously allowed RFK to have ownership for the idea as an act of support for RFK's political career.

Bolman, Lee G., and Terrence E. Deal. *Reframing Organizations.* San Francisco: Jossey-Bass, 1991.

Bridges, William. *Managing Transitions.* Reading, Mass.: Addison-Wesley, 1991.

Brooks, Michael. *The Power of Business Rapport.* New York: HarperCollins, 1991.

Buell, Barbara. "Businessland Seems Stuck in No-Man's-Land," *Business Week* (July 2, 1990).

Capra, Fritjof. *The Tao of Physics.* 2nd ed. Boston: New Science Library, 1985.

Carroll, Paul. *Big Blues: the Unmaking of IBM.* New York: Crown, 1993.

Chu, Chin-Ning. *The Asian Mind Game.* New York: Rawson Associates, 1991.

Collins, Larry, and Dominique Lapper. *Freedom at Midnight.* New York: Avon Books, 1975.

Douillard, John. *Body, Mind and Sport.* New York: Harmony Books, 1994.

Dumaine, Brian. "Toughest Bosses," *Fortune* (October 18, 1993).

Farnham, Alan. "State Your Values, Hold the Hot Air," *Fortune* (April 19, 1993).

Gergan, David. "Lip Balm for Bush," *U.S. News & World Report* (July 9, 1990).

Gilder, George. *Microcosm: The Quantum Revolution in Science and Technology.* New York: Simon and Schuster, 1989.

Goswami, Amit. *The Self-Aware Universe.* New York: Putnam, 1993.

Graves, Jacqueline M. "Leaders of Corporate Change," *Fortune* (December 14, 1992).

Greengard, S. "Eye for an Eye," *American Way* (April 1990).

Gross, Ronald. *Peak Learning.* Los Angeles: Tarcher, 1991.

Hamel, Gary, and C. K. Prahalad. *Competing for the Future.* Boston: Harvard Business School Press, 1994.

Heisenberg, Werner. *Physics and Philosophy.* New York: Harper, 1971.

Huey, John. "Managing in the Midst of Chaos," *Fortune* (April 5, 1993).

———. "America's Most Successful Merchant," *Fortune* (September 23, 1991).

Jenks, James M., and John M. Kelly. *Don't Do: Delegate!* New York: Ballantine, 1985.

Keller, Maryann. *Rude Awakening: The Rise, Fall, and Struggle for Recovery of General Motors.* New York: Morrow, 1989.

Koestenbaum, Peter. *Leadership: The Inner Side of Greatness.* San Francisco: Jossey-Bass, 1991.

Kroc, Ray. *Grinding It Out: The Making of McDonald's.* New York: Berkeley Medallion Books, 1977.

Labich, Ken. "Why Companies Fail," *Fortune* (November 14, 1994).

McCall, Morgan W., and Michael M. Lombardo. "What Makes a Top Executive?" *Psychology Today* (February 1983).

Mehrabian, Albert. *Silent Messages.* Belmont, Calif.: Wadsworth, 1971.

Nanus, Burt. *Visionary Leadership.* San Francisco: Jossey-Bass, 1990.

Pascale, Richard T. *Managing on the Edge.* New York: Touchstone, 1991, p. 114.

Penrose, Roger. *The Emperor's New Mind.* New York: Penguin Books, 1989. Penrose argues that consciousness is needed when we face "non-algorithmic" situations, i.e., situations that require characteristics such as common sense, judgment, understanding, and artistic appraisal. Penrose also argues that consciousness is not needed when situations are automatic, programmed, or dictated by rules that can be mindlessly followed. He explains the need for consciousness in the leadership arena, in the unpredictable situations where no established guidelines exist.

Peters, Tom, and Nancy Austin. *A Passion for Excellence.* New York: Random House, 1985.

————, and Robert Waterman. *In Search of Excellence.* New York: Harper, 1982.

Phillips, Don T. *Lincoln on Leadership: Executive Strategies for Tough Times.* New York: Warner Books, 1992.

Pritchard, Peter. *The Making of McPaper: The Inside Story of USA Today.* New York: St. Martin's Press, 1987.

Ray, Michael. "The New Business Paradigm," *New Traditions in Business,* ed. J. Renesch. San Francisco: Berrett-Koehler, Publishers, 1992.

————, and Rochelle Myers. *Creativity in Business.* New York: Doubleday, 1986.

Reich, Robert B. *The Work of Nations: Preparing Ourselves for 21st Century Capitalism.* New York: Knopf, 1991.

Rice, Faye. "Champions of Communications," *Fortune* (June 3, 1991).

Robbins, Anthony. *Unlimited Power.* New York: Fawcett Columbine, 1986.

————. *Awaken the Giant Within.* New York: Summit Books, 1991.

Saporito, Bill. "A Week Aboard the Wal-Mart Express," *Fortune* (August 24, 1992).

Schein, Edgar H. *Organizational Culture and Leadership.* San Francisco: Jossey-Bass, 1990.

Schlesinger, Arthur. *A Thousand Days.* Greenwich, Conn.: Fawcett Publications, 1965, pp. 756–757.

Secord, Paul F. "The Role of Facial Features in Interpersonal Perception," *Person Perception and Interpersonal Behavior,* eds. R. Tagiuri and L. Petrullo. Stanford, Calif.: Stanford University Press, 1958, pp. 300–315.

Senge, Peter. *The Fifth Discipline.* New York: Doubleday, 1990.

Sherman, Stratford. "Leaders Learn to Heed the Voice Within," *Fortune* (August 22, 1994).

Stewart, Thomas. "The King Is Dead," *Fortune* (January 1, 1993).

Swanson, Gerald, and Robert Oates. *Enlightened Management.* Fairfield, Ia.: MIU Press, 1989.

Taylor, Alex III. "Why Toyota Keeps Getting Better and Better," *Fortune* (November 19, 1990).

Thompson, Charles. *What a Great Idea!* New York: HarperCollins, 1992.

Tichy, Noel M., and Mary Anne Devanna. *The Transformational Leader.* New York: Wiley, 1990.

Townsend, Robert. *Up the Organization.* Greenwich, Conn.: Fawcett Publications, 1970.

Tully, Shawn. "Why Go for Stretch Targets?" *Fortune* (November 14, 1993).

Vaill, Peter. *Managing as a Performing Art.* San Francisco: Jossey-Bass, 1989.

von Oech, Roger. *A Whack on the Side of the Head.* New York: Warner Books, 1983.

Wallace, Robert Keith. *The Physiology of Consciousness.* Fairfield, Ia.: MIU Press, 1993.

Wheatley, Margaret J. *Leadership and the New Science.* San Francisco: Berrett-Koehler, 1992.

Wooden, John. *They Call Me Coach.* Waco, Tex.: Word Books, 1972.

Zohar, Danah. *The Quantum Self.* New York: Morrow, 1990.

Zukav, Gary. *The Dancing Wu Li Masters.* New York: Bantam Books, 1980.

Zuker, Elaina. *The Seven Secrets of Influence.* New York: McGraw-Hill, 1991.

Index